Lodestone

Hannah Stone

Stairwell Books
//

Published by Stairwell Books
70 Barbara Drive
Norwalk
CT 06851 USA

161 Lowther Street
York, YO31 7LZ

ISBN: 978-1-939269-42-3

Lodestone: Second Printing

Printed and bound in UK by Russell Press
Layout design: Alan Gillott
Cover Photograph: Suzanne Owen

For Simon

Acknowledgements and Notes

Many thanks are due to Suzanne Owen and Rosemary Mitchell, colleagues who walked the Stanza Stones trail with me in 2013 and encouraged me to become Hannah Stone; to Gill Lambert, who workshopped many of these poems during our MA workshops; to the writing community in Leeds, Harrogate and York with whom I have shared spoken word events and to Rose Drew and Alan Gillott of Stairwell Books for their enthusiasm and professionalism in producing this collection. Particular thanks are due to my poetry tutors on the MA in Creative Writing at Leeds Trinity University, Amina Alyal and Oz Hardwick. Their poetry enriches me, their feedback has helped me develop a voice and their unstinting help has been instrumental in my evolution as a writer. The volume is dedicated to Simon Coton, the best friend anyone could wish for, whose unflagging hospitality at his home in Llwyn Onn and companionship on holidays especially at Strumble Head supported most of the 'West' selection of this collection.

(S)hero resulted from a workshop with Sophie Nicholl on writing from the wild woods of the unconscious, Leeds Trinity University Writers' Festival, 2015.

Misnomer: the collective noun for peewits is "a deceit".

Doubletake and *Drip Feed* were published in *Caught in the Net* Issue 130, (http://www.poetrykit.org), April 2014. *Doubletake* was published in *Extraordinary Forms*, ed. Joy Howard (Grey Hen Publications, Keighley, 2016).

Humphrey Head, Gledhow Swan Upping, Intelligent Design, North Front, Floor Four, Sound Track, Silence in Court, Cormorant and *Tyddewi Revisited* were published in my Wordspace Pamphlet, *Perfect Timing*, on Createspace, March 2014. The 'found' element in *Cormorant* is from Collins *Colour Book of Birds*.

Cleveland Haiku are dedicated to Linda Walsh, my companion on the Cleveland Way.

Quizzical was published in *Hinterland Journal of Contemporary Poetry*, on 6 December 2013 under the title 'Your last cup of coffee'.

Buzz Off was chosen by Billy Collins to win the Yorkshire Poetry Prize in the Poetry Business Book and Pamphlet Competition, 2014-5 and published in *The North*, Issue 54.

The place names mentioned in *Stone* are from the OS maps of the Stanza Stones trail in N. Yorkshire.

Case Endings was published in *An After Dinner's Sleep*, with Gill Lambert and Maria Preston, ed. Oz Hardwick (Indigo Dreams Publishing, Beaworthy, 2015).

Dethroned and *Self Portrait, with Machete* (as *Losing your Head*) were published on poesiaindignada.com on 29 November 2014.

Reunion of the Broken Parts and *Overtime* were published on poesiaindignada.com on 30 June 2015.

The 'found' element in *Collateral Damage* is 'Lions at Antwerp Zoo shot': *The Times*, 9 October, 1914.

Reunion of the Broken Parts is the definition of the Arabic word al-jebr, according to *The Times*, 9 January, 2015. The quotation from Omar Khayyàm is from verse 51 of his *Rubaiyàt*.

The 'found' element in *Umm Hoda* is 'Sisa Abu Saooh – Egyptian woman who lives as a man – voted 'best mum'. *Guardian*, 23 March, 2015.

The 'found' element in *Overtime* refers to 'Brimob: teams of executioners appointed to carry out the death penalty on drugs-related convicts on the prison island of Nusa Kambangan, Indonesia'. *Guardian*, 7 March 2015.

Credo was published in *New Crops from Old Fields: Eight Medievalist Poets*, ed. Oz Hardwick (Stairwell Books, York, 2015).

Land Ahoy owes its genesis to words engraved on grey slate plaque at Abercastle Harbour: 'Alfred 'Centennial' Johnson, First Single Handed Atlantic Sailing West to East in a Fishing Dory, Gloucester, Mass, USA to Abercastle, Wales, June 15th – August 10th, 1876.'

The *Last Invasion* Tapestry may be found in the Civic Centre in Fishguard, Pembrokeshire.

Table of Contents

NORTH

(S)hero

A bear comes lumbering from the dark woods.
Her ribs rattle under matted fur.
Her belly tells her she must eat
if she is to feed the cubs who'll cling to her teats
in the longer days, but she is uncertain
about this young light that presses itself onto her eyes.

A wolf emerges, in another north,
smelling thaw-water flowing under the ice.
Her paws pick up last year's track
and the pack joins with her rhythm.
Above them the moon's pale disc
is a seed about to burst.

The woman stirs beneath crumpled sheets.
Wild, mammalian lines, which have tussled all night,
nudge her awake; this is archetype,
not Goethe's 'eternal feminine'
but a breathless *YES* to words' weight pressing to be birthed,
then slithering vigorously down bloodied thighs.

Three Peaks

I. Pen y Ghent

So, cantankerous hill, now you present
a proud profile, etching
your features onto grey sky,
mezzotint in monochrome.
Yet three hours ago, your contours
engraved themselves on my thigh muscles,
and a white veil draped your shapeliness.

Sitting barefoot, glass of wine in hand,
I scan you from across the valley.
At first, sunset tints your peaks,
smooths out a dimension, re-inscribes
a silhouette. The evening light
reshapes your boldness, then night
shades the slopes.

II. Almost Equinox, Ingleborough

The road swings right and there you are –
bold as a punk at a garden party,
strutting your snowy plume, old flat top,
your flank studded with sunlight,
while the crew-cut hedges at your knees
sell out to the new season's greens,

snowdrops spat out on the verge
subversive accessories to the act.

III. Whernside

The northern gods do things differently.

Jonah's wrathful Yahweh
cast his shrinking violet
into the belly of a whale,
sent petty worms
to destroy his hopes of shelter.

The Vanir of gods does business here,
borrowing the shape of a whale,
and bidding this hill shrug its shoulders
through layers of limestone.

Millstone grit pierces the clouds,
and puny Ninevites prick its slopes
with walking poles,

offer blocks
of Kendal mintcake. ⁄⁄

Volunteer

Did you call a taxi? jokes the driver,
lumbering out of his pickup. A grouse
snickers; I laugh and slurp coffee.
I'm not feeding them, he says.
Listen how they chatter
now the shooting season's done!
No, I'm here for moley; checking my traps.

One hand dangles the cut-off-their-tails blade,
the other presents the sad, flat pouch
of a small engineer, who helped construct
the Dales metrosystem,
blind miles of earthern tunnels
that route listeria into the valley haycrop.

Counting the cost, the moleman comes on Sunday
mornings,
to tease open the flaps he's carved.
Gouts of earth slide off the knife
he plunges into the mossy bank.
This limp, velvet scrap, snub-snouted,
seems such a small slice of the economy. ⁄⁄

Doubletake

Mindfuck you might call it –
technically, cognitive dissonance. First, the place,
a cottage garden hugging the moorland path,
where he shudders as he beats the bounds,
spinning his fantail like a disco-ball,
wafting with shapely feathers an indifferent peahen,
his urgent hoarseness the solo
to a backing track of curlews and larks.
   She's unimpressed – seen it before –
but look again – no turquoise eye
is shimmering on a bronzed plume.
Perhaps the Pennine rain has bled him dry
for every feather's innocent of tint,
and like the sky's broad colourchart of greys
so he displays each variant of white,
of clouds, of cottongrass, of milk,
spume rising from the stream
or mist plunging down from the hillside.
   He's trembling, striving to keep it up:
still he gyrates, still she ignores
his desperate pride, the hunger
for her plump, ordinary brownness.

Misnomer

Nothing deceptive but your duality of names,
one of which renders, reductively, your call,
onomatopoeic note of how you scissor the air
into grey streamers of spring fog.

The other voices timid words,
'lap' and 'wing' as feeble attempts
to pin down your courtship's wild spiralling.
You're nature's anarchists, de-stabilising the system,

mocking the laws of physics as you hurtle
towards the impregnable field,
your dare-devil ride playing dodgems with hard ground.
The Alphas relaunch to the top of the helter-skelter.

Behind the barriers, bound by convention,
we're jealous spectators of your dodge and swerve.
The gate we're leaning on dictates:
Under no circumstances should your vehicle leave the track.

Humphrey Head

Hungry, angry, loping to the furthest rim
of earth-meets-sky, the last grey wolf hunkers down.
His grizzled muzzle's stained
with recent chicken kill, teeth bared in rictus.

Righteous and brutal, but just as scared,
the hunter squats low in the reedbed.
He catches the feral smell of something
driven wilder to the edge of contested land.

Where should he seek? Inland, behind the leaning swathes
of trees, a lone thornbush steering into the wind,
each foot of rock kaleidoscoped with lichen
sharing the last foothold above the tideline.

Or facing outwards, back to the dense earth,
moving from solid to shifting, from stone to beguiling strands
neither sand not mud nor water but all three
silting and shimmering.

Sea-birds deposit webbed prints
as they dart across the elements
but neither the wolf nor the man has wings. ⁄⁄

Four Cleveland Haiku

I

forging day from night
seagulls hammer summer skies
sculpt hiccupping cries

II

adder lifts her head
latent energy
coiled under harvest sunshine

III

elemental trick
wind woven with wolfish cries
seals hold court off shore

IV

clouds of butterflies
escape through swathes of bracken
trampled flat by boots ⁄⁄

Location, Location, Location

Herring Heights is a high-spec penthouse suite in an enviable location on top of the sole remaining rock stack to the east of the popular Lebbeston Cliff area. Competitively priced, this stunning coastal property offers development opportunities for an energetic family of up-and-coming gulls ambitious to move up the property ladder. Elegantly appointed with sandstone floors and low maintenance roofgarden, Herring Heights would make an ideal home for the outdoorsy type, with shared fishing access a mere 80 feet below (no permit required under Yorkshire Wold Regeneration Scheme). Sea breezes ensure complete comfort in even the warmest conditions. Viewing essential. ✐

Full survey recommended in light of reported subsidence in the vicinity.

Tide Tables

The priory is a grave never closed to the elements,
where faded notices inform tourists of opening hours,
and nanny-state placards warn irrepressible children
against the perils of climbing stairs that lead
to no-where very much, but it passes the time
till they queue for ice-creams.

In its day, monastic hours sculpted the daylight
into blocks for different tasks; so much for prayer, study;
a short sleep before lauds, another before matins.
In summer, the elastic hours stretched
like the coastline, shimmering into distance.
In winter, darkness squashed the days,
lengthened nights too drafty for sleep.

But the sea of faith found new channels,
a riptide of reformers roared its way
across the land, fast and furious
as the hooves of horses galloping now on Bamburgh beach,
giving the holiday riders a thrill.
The monastery became a quarry for local builders,
and the wind chewed away at the remains,
fiddling the sandstone walls into a filigree
as fine as any Fabergé curio.

Where once a smudgy tallow glow
illuminated incantations, sunlight hovers,
and a sparrow flies, shouldering the gusts,
which waft buddleia's honey scent
into an empty chancel.
The bird picks its way up a ragged wall,
now rooved only by scudding clouds,
takes sanctuary in a crevice
where its tiny eye shares the perspective of masons
who hewed, then shaped, the umber chunks,
skilled men spending a lifetime with rough hands,
maybe even giving life itself,
to build this island home for prayer.

Now, the monks' offices have given way
to tidetables; the ordered pace
of contemplation overtaken by metered slots
for shopping, beach-combing, maybe
the lighting of a candle if there's time
before the parking permit runs out
and the causeway sinks again. ⁄⁄

Treasure Trove

Despite some scattered litter
(empty drink tins, bottle tops,
one stained and stranded trainer)
this beach seems untenanted for now,
the perfect place for a visiting hermit
to scuttle beneath a newspaper
for a restful hour or two.

A gull's klaxon call alerts my ears. Uncovered,
eyes screwed shut against a sudden gritty wind
peel open. On duty now, sight
makes sense of shape.

Across the cove, ten stone pyramids
suggest an artisan's activity –
these are no random remnants
flung by the waves which embroider the shoreline
with ribbons of smelly weed,
but careful selection, with flat flanges
forming the bases for rounded mounds,
sizes, shapes, textures chosen for effect.

Did one pair of hands alone
mould this Andy Goldsworthy homage,
or is this a flow, a flood of imitation?
I think the latter, as I, too, grapple
the cold, wet weights, balancing and stacking
in obedience to the primal impulse
to sift order from chaos,
defying the tide's own ceaseless act of grace. ⁄⁄

Bad Dog, Good Hair Day

Ok, so I bitched on Facebook about the dogs,
especially that bundle of angry fur
that shot out of the woods
and fastened itself to my leg
(not for copulatory purposes),
the sort of small, yappy beast
you want to slide your toe under,
to boot into the sky
with a cartoon YELP! and SPLAT!

But I also want to record the day's wonders,
that strands of honeysuckle were still in flower,
trailing their long bells of sweetness
through tangled wet leaves,
and how I caught unawares a flock of geese,
a hundred or more, standing to attention
as if they'd been given the heads-up
about the second coming.

I want to recall that this season's glut of ladybirds
is not your common red spotty type,
but an elegant breed of black with white cheeks,
and that one flexed his enamelled wing-cases on my knee,
and that a dozen sparrows rose on a single wingbeat
and, chorusing briefly, stored themselves in the hedge.

And I loved the wind fingering my hair,
and the warm breeze on my skin, and I laughed
at the guy vainly raising his zoom lens
to snap the red kite's teasing display.
I marvelled at the sun silvering
the wet blades of grass.

I knew it was altogether a good hair day
when I sat back down at my desk,
and a spider abseiled past my ear
and landed on the keyboard. ⁄⁄

Quizzical

Your last cup of coffee was

A double espresso from Starbucks, at Bank tube station,
six thirty am, en route to a breakfast meeting, patting
your cashmere suit to check
the datastick with your powerpoint presentation.

Sweet and milky, brought to you on the oncology ward
by the night sister who remembers
that Mrs Smith's daughter prefers it to tea.

Black, instant, drunk standing up in the kitchen
while texting your BFF about last night's date, LOL.
Alka Seltzer chaser.

Abandoned in the bedroom
while you looked for your daughter's PE kit,
pulled up your jeans and lobbed the carkeys at your
partner,
who'd left them under his socks on the floor.

Savoured in the garden, from a cracked mug
leaning on a sunny bench and serenaded
by a blackbird. Soil rimming your nails. ⁄⁄

Resurrection

Long ago winter storms flattened the fence,
allowing a fox to own the gap on the boundary
between next door's garden and mine,
a feeding station on his suburban circuit.

He'd pause on my lawn, snaffle up
the scrapings off the cats' plates,
and scraps of bacon put down for the birds.
My neighbour's rose spilled fragrant petals

over my currant bushes; brambles colonised
the no-man's land between our plots.
The damson tree behind my garage spread out,
distributing its fruit impartially.

But now my neighbour has grandchildren to rein in:
the cry of a newborn splits the air; toddlers
call for my friendly cat through the tangled stems.
It's time to fix the fence, says granddad.

The expansive tree, the fox's route,
are in the way of posts and panels
that will keep the children
safely penned in place.

From my study I hear the screaming
of the circular saw as it fells
the innocent intruder before it fruits again.
We slice it into firewood, stack it in the store.

Three weeks later, I go to fetch kindling
and see from green buds on lopped branches
forgiving blossoms are blooming,
and inhale the sharp foxy odour. ⁄⁄

Call of Nature

Hello? I'm returning your call,
Sorry I missed you. I know I said
I'd be in all day but ... pause to
search mental and moral pockets
for excuses and euphemisms ...
I was temporarily indisposed.

No, that won't do. She'll think
I'd gone for a pee, or was showering
after impromptu sex.

Truth was I went into the garden
to pull up the first radish of the month,
its bold pink curves breasting the soil,
a smooth, bright shape between earth and leaf,
enticing to the eye. I tug it up,
twist off the leaves, rinse the roots
in a handy puddle – oh!
the crispness, the tangy bite in my mouth!
But as I reach for another I hear it,
that perky phoney ringtone
calling me back on duty just too late.

Hello? Thank you for calling.
I'm here now, if you want to try again? ⁄⁄

Bramble

To pick this fruit requires courage.
You must push your hand into the maw of the bush,
oblivious to the fine fangs which greet you.
Even the least ambitious will feel driven
to reach ever higher for the plumpest prizes,
those sun-swollen fruits basking overhead
for which you will pay with a barcode of scratches
from elbow to white shoulder.
Fingers become blooded
by the obsessive greed of the eyes
and your belly knows
the blackbird needs to share
the gleanings of this harvest.

Drowned Frog

One of your native elements has done for you.
Though every ligament reached for soft air,
the rain which filled the bucket overnight
has stopped your spring.

Extending your symmetry upon the path
proved futile; nothing could shift the flow
that flooded your lungs. All that's left
is a flightless arrow, pointing to the hedge.

Come the next downpour, ants
will have cleaned your bones of flesh,
your pin-fine skeleton mapping the small deaths
that even a shower can bring. ⁄⁄

Gledhow Swan Upping

Last month three adolescent cygnets ducked their heads,
embarrassed by my interest,
and cob and pen circled their brood
with arching necks and coiled wings.
Now two offspring alone remain,
emboldened, perhaps, by the sudden spillage
of growth down the hillside, where bonsai versions
of good green things begin to top the soil,
beguiling the stubborn snow with promises
of celandines, feathery fronds of wood anemones,
and flat blades of bluebells, ramsons, cuckoopint
in promiscuous proximity.

And the dogwalker's accent
conveys an authority at odds with her grimy jacket -
she thinks our missing fledgling's a boy,
that 'dad' has seen him off
so he can 'have another go at mum.'

Unmated now, I yet recall a time
when pairing meant for keeps,
and what I've kept from then I will not lose.
Unlike these swans, no male possessor
will drive away my boys
because the breeding season's come again.

Walking home on ripening soil, my warm breath
ascends in frosty homage to the dryads;
offering thanks for green-ness, sunshine,
thawing snow, wet dogs, wild birds
and gloriously free range sons. ⁄⁄

Buzz Off

For some days now bees have shared
the airbrick in my study. Tomorrow
a field biologist arrives to identify,
pacify, and remove them from my life.

I envisage him calming them to sleep
with puffs of smoke then carefully
taking a soft brush and sweeping
the dozing creatures
into a large canvas sheet, like the one
the apostle Peter saw in a vision,
lowered from heaven, containing an arkful
of all God's four footed beasts.

I wonder if while he is about it
the biologist (or maybe some cosmic exterminator)
could brush my room clean of God,
collecting each vituperative doctrine
(the sting of original sin and
foul stench of misogyny)
and drop them into the hanging cloth,
prodded where necessary by tiny demons
who have stolen their pitchforks from Hieronymous Bosch.

But in the evening having cleaned
the smears of honey off the wall
I find the Almighty
curled on my sofa between the cats
like the old friend who forgets to leave after dinner
sending me yawning into the kitchen
for a second pot of coffee, wishing I could
extinguish the candle and pad upstairs
accompanied by purring companions
and no sense of guilt. ⁄⁄

Instructions to the Poet from a Magic Realist

Imagine yourself as a butterfly,
with an anvil awaiting your return.
Start each day allowing wind to billow
beneath your wings.
Alight on promising blooms;
sip succour from their sweetness,
but guard against giddiness
from sugar highs and sunshine.

As darkness falls, steer towards your forge.
There, deposit each drop of nectar.
Allow it to set, then hammer into shapes.
Apply heat: once malleable
challenge their pretence,
remould them into less artful forms.
Plunge your new draft into cold water,
then examine dispassionately
the rough edges, the textures
of the words you have linked.

Place on the workbench of the mind while you sleep.

You snooze, you lose, Colin!

I loathe this woman, who's paid
by a chain of 'leisure hotels'
to interrupt my viewing, punctuating
with her chummy bullying the narrative
of my chosen detective drama,
its splashy Cornish scenery and gritty characters.
I hate her bright 'n' breezy manner,
the way she pushes to the front
of every cupcake queue, haranguing
her shadowy mate without dimming her kilowatt smile.

Frankly, I'd rather the static nylon sheets
and dripping shower of the cruddiest b and b
than a night in the hotel she advertises.
Imagine going down to breakfast
in yesterday's walking kit
(which passed the sniff test)
and finding her at the buffet,
fresh and tangy as the fruit platter, rolling
her over-painted eyes at waiters
chosen for exotic but unthreatening ethnicity.

I'd lurk at the back of the pack with Colin the loser,
dragging our heels behind her Jimmy Choos.
We'd pile too many sausages on our plates,
and plunge the coffee clumsily,
a fountain of granules caffeinating the cloth.
With luck, he'll wake one morning
and find she was just a bad dream; better still,
he'll stir, peer over the edge
of the kingsize moraine of pallid sheets,
and discover her lifeless body splattered on the shagpile,
and find a heavy blunt object clasped in his sleepy hand. //

Intelligent Design

Upgrading from plank-between-pallets
to a proper woodcutter's bench,
squatting, sweating in the act of creation,
screwdriver and wrench to hand
and, having fixed the cross bars (fig. 3) onto the legs (fig. 5),
I'm musing over the plastic caps
("Stretch tautly over leg ends") and wondering
at just which minute of which hour on the sixth day
God dreamed up the kid's skid-proof hoof
and how many begattings of goats it took
to perfect the angle of their grip. ⁄⁄

Stone

Beck spins the axis of a line of stones
marching across the horizon,
conscripts them into vertical columns, funnelling
the unstoppable in its task of transformation.

High Stones, Doe Stones,
Rocking Stone, Pancake Stone,
Great Skirtful of Stones.

Stony Edge Flat.

Stone walls make good fences make good neighbours;
this plumbline of water new thresholds
between form and chaos; stones swelling lichenslow
beneath tussock and heather,
erupting from moorland as sheepfold,
cottage, flagged path striding
past Robin Hood's Bed.

West Buck Stones, Doubler Stones,
Cup and Ring marked stones,
Swastika Stone, Noon Stone.

Aiggin Stone.

Stones are marshalled as harbours
for the flotsam from the mind's Sargasso Sea,
a name to build with, foundations not on sand.

Blackstone Edge, Millstone Edge,
Rook Stones Hill,Lady Blantyre's Rock.

Stanza Stones. ⁄⁄

SOUTH

Third Dog

I am no *Pictor Ignotus*, indeed I share
the famed name of brother and father.
The youngest of the three Luinis,
I'm spending all summer in Milan,
striving to keep the walls of S. Maurizio
as sodden as our sweat-drenched, paint-splattered shirts;
lunging at the sinopia with stubby brushes,
coaxing from smeary palettes
bright images, landscapes, people
to narrate the Bible stories for the nuns.
Strange alchemy that parables
derive shape and form from our hands!
Our painting's blessed by the church,
funded by men hungry for notice.
The bubble reputation's blown from fat lips;
patrons scurry from confession
with one hand already dipping
into a velvet purse; what price
atonement for their lewdity?

In this job, you have to get down and dirty.
The mouldy lime and eggy stinks
crawl into your mouth by bedtime,
and when a thundery shower
steals the sunlight, then bring out candles
so you can finish the panel
while the plaster's still absorbent.
And I lie awake, these hot nights,
imagining lightning casting its mercurial flickering
on the tapered roof of the ark.
Maybe those herons are a bit too big
but this time they're my creation –
a whole section to show my craft!
I've served my time – yard after yard
of folded fabrics, skies, grasses
I've painted, taking instructions
from elders and betters; old farts

who cramp my style, giving me the dross
to fill in. It feels like painting by numbers,
while they of course touch up faces, shine the pearls –
the details that court flattery.

A jagged flash, then dark as pitch.
The sole giraffe waits in shadow
to meet his mate in the morning.
When we splash over the cobbles,
the door is swollen with rainfall
but the roof of the church
is sound as a bell, and the lads
are already there, kicking stones
at the pigeons. I cuff them inside, set them to work
grinding and blending the minerals –
all the chores I worked my young arse off doing.

Father and brother are busy
pressing the flesh, hunting contracts:
by the time they catch on to what I've done
the Noah story's all complete.
If I position myself just *here*
my sleeve will hide the extra dog,
my faithful mutt immortalised
in fresco for the nuns to see.
No glossy lapdog crouched in silks,
but a rough-haired mongrel,
this hound's surpassed in loyalty
any number of wives and pals:
a dog's a better friend to man,
and maybe Noah won't mind
a bit of extra company:
the wife's a shrew, by all accounts.

So here it is, my finished wall,
and though I may not sign my name
those in the know will recognize
the single disembodied head,
rising from the grass, sign of our confraternity.
Se prega di non toccare,
but let my painting speak to you. ⁄⁄

Drip Feed

Why you here reading accused an unsummoned
philosopher
clad in nihilistic black.
Dark, too, was his dogma – we'll all heading for that drip
at the end of your life, they plug you in
that drip
salt and water cos we came out of the ocean
we need the water, he proclaims, warming to his theme,
leaning
as if into the wind.

Gusts of breakfast cider belch into my face.

We came craving the sugar of the land
not just the salt and water, so why
you reading, what's your script;
all the money's in videos now, you wasting
your time, he shouts
making it sound like I've filched minutes –
hours even – from the store of his
coffee-spooned day.

Why you bother, he finishes
and the small craft in his angry mind
tacks off as he lurches
into the unresponsive ocean of Russell Square.
And still I wait for the library to open,
the harbour towards which I pilot
my flimsy bobbing vessel, reaching up
to impale myself on the cannula
of the printed page,
the slow drip-feed of other people's knowledge
filling my veins for a shift or two,
a quick fix, a sugar high, before oblivion. ⁄⁄

North Front, Floor Four

Sometimes while I'm here I visit my first book,
immaculately conceived in such a place,
cells dividing into conference papers
and chapter drafts; the birth bloodless,
leaving no stretch-marks.
An undemanding infant, requiring
no new shoes or orthodontics.

Often I find her snuggled between
"Cyprus from 1191-1374"
and a festschrift for Brenda Bolton,
whose black and white cat
resented posing as partial proof
of the 'human face' of scholarship.

Once when I called she was out.
My heart pricked - well, hermaphrodite,
are you even now fertilizing
a fresh young ovum of discovery
somewhere on the Backs, where swans
twist their necks into lovehearts for the tourists?

Sound Track

Pouring scorn on feeble female fumblings
with the sat nav, he suggests
I'm cartographically challenged, too,
not noticing how I'm led by music.
and thus I note my routes.
The A14 turn off the A1 is mostly
at seven and a half minutes into track one
of a certain something by Syd Barrett,
a last shared chord
with the student slumbering beside me,
harvesting his final hour of sleep
before the winter sowing.

Heading north again, safely delivered,
we're empty, the car and I.
Shine on, you crazy diamond,
sparkling in the misty fens.
My insurers must never know
I've been driving under the influence of Pink Floyd. ⁄⁄

Case Endings

This strange new tongue I have invited
into my mouth twists meaning,
its syntax delivering new intent –
'by me are two sons, students,'
the phrasebook dictates:
'one will become doctor, one lawyer,' it insists.

Today, my proto-lawyer holds court
in his fine blank space which fills up with
hoodies, computer, champagne flutes,
a case of beer, some books and poker chips
and other necessities of life.

Shoulder to shoulder we embrace;
a patch of cheek which escaped
your hasty morning razor
abrades my ear;

then voices of friends to be
clatter along the corridor,
follow me downstairs,

voices of strangers in the car demand
I order 'tea with milk', 'a room with a bath'.

Above the motorway a glider trawls for peace

as men sing prayers to their father
in some English cathedral

petitioning for health, wisdom, light
on this improbably bright October evening -
perhaps a kind, strong father

not the threat of a parent long hanging
dusty in the sombre closet of my youth
or the runaway dad who left
when your hugs barely reached my waist.

You've outgrown this casing now:
gym-honed pecs bursting
through your clothes like Tom Kitten,
your man's voice crowds out the treble reed;
a crumpled beer can lies beside the bed.

Tucking rubles into my passport
I rehearse the phrases,
re-translate; from me were two sons,
who live in different cities:
they will become themselves.
Tomorrow, my turn to fly. ⁂

I Hope they Don't Eat Earthlings

Half an hour was all it took
to transform the flaky shapes
at the ends of my fingers
into glossy gems, equipping me
with ten enamelled tools. I stared
at the scalp of the acolyte to glamour
who bent his head over the ritual.
I hadn't expected a *man* to be one of them.

Obedient to his gestures, I slid my fingers
in and out of a buzzing portal
which emits an unearthly light.
With a dolls-house brush,
his hands, smaller than mine,
drew unfamiliar calligraphy on my extremities.
Occasionally, he and the others incanted Mandarin
as they transformed me into a new species:
the well-groomed woman about town.

That evening, addressing an audience,
my newly-decorated hands re-wrote my identity.
Hand gestures became self-conscious;
I fiddled with my necklace, stifled a simper.
When I awoke next morning,
I'd forgotten my transformation and startle myself
at the sight of these alien cling-ons.
I hope they don't eat earthlings. ⁄⁄

Sea Change

The first thing you relinquished was independence,
a graceful abdication granting small tasks
to nimbler fingers, swifter legs –
buttons to sew on, letters to post.

As weeks went by, pain took control.
Your world contracted to two rooms:
plants in the sitting room wanted watering,
and the glasstop table gathered dust.

When one room alone became your domain
we still found jobs to do,
sifting boxes of clip-on ear-rings
into glittering piles for the charity shop.

Urged to make a choice of something
to remember you by, I raised
strings of coral, threaded pearls,
held their chill against my neck.

Sometimes we rattled the mesh fence of death,
peered through its falseness, cried a little.
I brought you the scent of summer gardens
in a bunch of sweet peas.

After you've gone, the air here is stale,
though no longer heavy with waiting.
I jerk clots of milk down the sink,
switch off the fridge, rinse the dishcloths.

The estate agent rat-a-tat-tats
as I'm watering the spider plant
and dead-heading the African violet.
I ask her to put the empties on the step.

Digging Deep

Eighty-four in the shade, one September afternoon,
we're planting leek seedlings, my father and I.
I'm Janus-aged, both parent and child:
it's hard to say who's helping who today.

Hardened by years of submission
I sustain the posture of supplicant,
raising gloved hands to receive each green strand.
Soil is trapped in the white net of rootlets.

He demands correct observance
of the measuring stick and watering can,
as if placating this vegetable patch
could draw down some benediction on our lives.

As our hands touch and part
he talks, a litany interrupted
by treks to the waterbutt
and language wandering off.

Some words are easy to find:
these new pills might give me the runs
he confides, and mentions *alternatives*,
as if he could choose how to grow old.

Other phrases are as inaccessible
as the quinces high in the unpruned tree,
that drop aromatic plumpness
onto dry soil.

We sift flints and stones as we plant, wonder
if this sharp chunk might be an arrowhead.
He fumbles for the name of a cousin who collects *such things*.
For now, circumlocution will serve. ⟋

Dethroned

On 'good' days you stood in a sea of words,
arms powerless to save each wave
from washing further out of reach
the language on which your work set sail,
which flooded us in the family home.
You railed and swore with fragments still conscripted,
half-laughing when invention displaced memory.

I'd meet you halfway, on the shore of meaning.

Perhaps your 'bad' days now are preferable,
when your mouth chews on nothing,
and your eyes are empty;
I prompt you in my head:
*See, I cannot hold the tide,
not I, even I, with all my force.
Speak for me.*

What shall Cordelia speak? Love, and be silent.

Strata

Squat amber figurine,
a dagger in an ornate sheath,
doctor's birdbeak speculum:
treasured possessions carried
on the exodus from Pompeii.

Archaeologists debate what earthquakes displaced
and what looters disturbed later,
as they snatched their booty, scratching 'house tunnelled'
onto hardened lava. They assume the town
ossified embarrassment, panic
on that August night. They ask
why things are in the wrong place,
tradesmen's tools in the dining room,
and wealthy matrons in the gladiators' digs?

In the television age, the strata
in home counties' houses are less mysterious,
unambiguously dated. The flight from infirmity's a
stumbling
not from the swiftness of pyroclastic surge
but the glacial advance of confusion, weariness and horror.
Desk drawers contain payslips from 1958 -1983,
fifty three annual Rentokil contracts, guaranteeing a house
free from woodworm; a stash of used envelopes;
the daily entries in the carers' log: *left comfortable.*

The midden, if there had been one, would hold
less noble mementos: twenty seven unmatched socks,
a wastepaper basket used as a pissoir,
carpets stained and soiled.

Like their tourist visitors today, those southern people
loved to gawp at the exotic, the erotic;
ingenious phallic jokes drooping or thrusting
from table ware, hanging lamps, road signs:
symbols of the generative force which survived volcanoes
and might placate the gods.

In not-quite rural Surrey, the dust, less toxic, settles on evidence of mundane lapses no longer private; functions exposed, recorded.
Nothing is set in stone. ⁄⁄

Orans

Glancing into back gardens from the train
which bumps over the points near Herne Hill
I glimpse a man standing on a patio
eyes closed, hands uplifted.

He's wearing jeans, and a neat pullover
(it's chilly) – trainers, too, I think.
He's found a patch of sunlight
for his morning prayers.

I'd like a share in the peace
he's invoking, or whatever blessing
is channelled through palms fanned out
under the grubby sky. It seems

he has a connection with some god
up there, looking down
on sidings, fireweed and fleeting views
of faces peering through windows.

If I clothed him in saffron robes and sandals,
perfumed the spring air with ambergris,
laid soft grass beneath his feet
and wove a mountain breeze through his fingers,

would he select a deity for me,
preferably a compassionate type,
and suggest a mantra
to offer up from the Southern line?

EAST

Collateral Damage

It is a curious sensation, waiting.
Before dawn, the streets leading to the station,
to the gates on the north and west,
were crowded with fugitives, forlorn people,
dragging bundles, the wealthier citizens with bags, even
trunks.
This morning, the streets were in turmoil.
This afternoon, stragglers still go hurrying by.
There will be one more boat, leaving tonight:
it is a curious sensation, waiting.

I went to the famous Restaurant du grand Laboureur for
lunch; the cook had fled, but the patron made me an
omelette, which the solitary remaining waiter served with
the aid of a single boy. I understand there will be one more
boat leaving tonight, but I do not know if it is true.
Thereafter, those who are left in the city will, presumably,
only get out by walking to the Dutch frontier.

The post and telegraph offices are closed.
The public bureaus have shut their doors.
Business is suspended, bombardment expected
at any moment. It was due at ten o'clock this morning.
Apparently the enemy has not yet got his large guns
into satisfactory position. Harbingers have reached
the inner forts. He can reach the centre of the town
at almost any minute.
It is a curious sensation, waiting.

Curiosity took me to the admirable Zoological Gardens;
there I saw one of the saddest sights of the war – a great,
gaping grave, containing four splendid lions lying in it, still
limp from life. They had been shot, lest in the course of the
bombardment their cages should be broken, and they
should get out. I spoke to the man with the rifle, who was on
his way to kill other dangerous carnivora. I spoke to the
director of the gardens, and they both choked with sorrow
as they talked.

They should get out.
The Director of the Gardens,
the Burgomaster,
the General Commanding,
the solitary remaining waiter,
the single boy,
the man with the rifle,
the dangerous carnivora,
the four splendid lions –
they should get out.

It is a curious sensation, waiting. ⁄⁄

Undone

In midlife a spider crawls over a woman's body
laying down webs between her breasts,
clouding with fine filaments the corners of her eyes;
the sharp edge of her cheek becomes blunted,
the smooth paleness of her hands
rots into mottling.

In the ninth year of the war
a soldier lifts his head to peer
through blooded eyeholes of a helmet
glimpsing a woman not uncomely (and wellbred)

but, truth be told, in the dark reaches of the night,
it is not her form which stiffens his prick
but the thought of his serving wench
bending smooth haunches over her pots of oil
in a shady corner of the storeroom.

And as he hears the whistling progress of the spear
that will pin him to the ground
he wonders whether it was the face of Helen
that had driven them on – all the fathers bereft,
the wives desolated, sons unsired by carnage –
or rather the act of possession,
that ancient hunger that drives men to war
without regret or indecision until

at the final gasp
the hands each soldier craves
are not those of their fine wives and willing whores
but the uncunning clasp
of the woman who gave him suck,
whose face has been veiled
by the spinnings of time. ⁄

Sekhmet, Museo Egizio di Torino

Like the mummies in nearby cases
you conceal a half-life beneath
a complex, crafted surface.
Electric light bounces off the blue-black planes
of your lidless eyes, your vast arms and belly,
cold flares, as if the sun-disc
poised on your head were nearly eclipsed.

Your lioness heart lies under
shy, decorative buds of breasts,
savage rage tainting your human milk.

Mighty goddess, you store healing powers
in a basket woven of fire and venom;
in you, benevolent Hathor becomes vengeful,
restoration and destruction turn on each other,
two serpents sewn into a sack
and entombed in basalt. ⫽

Umm Hoda

I'm used to wearing men's clothes now:
it's forty years since I last revealed
any feminine curves: back in the seventies
concealment was the only way
to keep new suitors at bay.
My husband passed away three months before
our daughter was born, and my brothers
were desperate to marry me off again,
make me somebody else's wife
before I'd even mourned my first man
or given life to our child.

What choice did I have? I'd not been to school,
but I had the strength of ten men!
I shaved my hair off, chose loose-fitting robes because
manual labour was the only way
I could provide for my daughter –
making bricks, harvesting wheat – anything
the men could do, I'd turn my hand to.

I disappeared from view,
though I never pretended
to be what I wasn't. In time,
the whole of Luxor knew about me.
Umm Hoda they called me, Hoda's Mum.

Umm Hoda gave up more than skirts.
I had to learn to think like a man;
that way, they accepted me as one of them.
After work we'd all go and drink coffee together.
No-one bothered me because I'd put aside
my femininity; back home, my brothers never forgave me.

Am I still labouring, you ask?
Well, these days I'm not so strong as I was,
so I've taken up shining shoes,
and the city chiefs gave me a kiosk

to shelter me from the weather!
I don't mind what I do, as long as Hoda
doesn't have to do what Hoda's mum does.
Her man's too ill to work, so now
I'm helping out so *her* kids can eat.

It was a proud moment when the President
shook my hand and gave me the award
for being the most devoted mum.
One day, when I get time, I'll ask Hoda
to read me everything that's written
on the gilt-edged certificate. ⁄⁄

Overtime

Pulling the trigger's the easy part, because
you never know if it's actually you
or one of the other Brimob officers
who's firing live rounds. It might be
that I've never fired a fatal shot!

We work in a team, five of us to fetch
the prisoner from his isolation cell.
They don't protest much, though –
they've been on death row long enough.
It takes place in the middle of the night.
If it were light enough, maybe you'd see
more than the whites of their eyes.
They can choose to cover their face
before we tie them up.

That's the worst bit; touching
men who are about to die,
lacing their hands and feet and limbs
to the cross, using thick rope. God has decreed
whether or not they sin. I say to them:
I'm sorry, just doing my job.

It's extra cash, you see – we're police officers by day.
We get $100 a time for this, by way of bonus, earn it
for those few moments of brutal intimacy –
the sweaty palms and rapid breathing. We escort them
to a clearing in the jungle.

In the darkness, a torch is shone
onto a target drawn over their hearts.
You could cover it with the palm of your hand.

In my nightmares I am dazzled
by that beam, but stare into it
for as long as I can, because when it drops
below my gaze, I know my brothers are taking aim.

51

Reunion of the Broken Parts

Social media swiftly shifts awareness.
One minute *je suis Charlie* swamps the screens,
then someone tweets that Ahmed
was gunned down defending the right
of atheists to ridicule his God.
Does he get seventy-two virgins, too?

Facebook is flooded with homage cartoons:
a snapped pencil sharpens itself, twice.
*The moving finger writes, and having writ
Moves on*; now, *je suis juif*,
and holocaust memorial day
raises its grizzled head once more.

Meanwhile, in Saudi Arabia
a blasphemer receives fifty
of his allocated thousand lashes.
Who can find one deity to hold it all together
while his flayed back begins to knit,
and someone posts *je suis Bartholemew*?

Self-Portrait, With Machete

In the old days there was much smiting.
Old Masters showed burly arms raised seconds
before the scourge dropped, deadweight
on the unribboned back of Christ.

Frescoes froze forever Salome's sly smile
at her dangling trophy,
the baptizer's neck spangling
Tuscan hillsides with ruby pigment.

A Pre-Raphelite painted More's head
lowered by soldiers, in a basket;
no pot of Basil for Margaret, but
tearful embalming in soft cloth.

Now, a triumphal jihadist poses
against the concrete of Raqqua's square,
tweeting *Chillin' with my homie
or what's left of him*. Hashtag showed him.

Grey light filters through the chainlink;
he hides his own head from the sun's eye
and the world's gaze; not much left
of his humanity. ⁄⁄

Mickelgarth, 2014

I. Ataturk Airport

The transit lounge is a glazed case
displaying lines of travellers, snapped
in a shutter-click, halted for a moment
while they wait to pass from here to there,
inhabitants of multiple continents sliding
from one time zone to another.
The afternoon ticks on as flights take off.

My curiosity controls the lens;
I blink again, they come to life.
They have drooping moustaches
or trim goatees and shaved heads,
tight pants and bare midriffs
or saggy skirts swaddling slumped bellies,
shades pushed up on botoxed foreheads
or brows modestly covered – head cloths
transparent, ornate, short, encompassing –
naked feet tucked up under hips,
or bare toes poking from two-tone stilettos
teetering beneath clingfilm tight dresses
and pouting cupid's bows.

Boys scatter like marbles as their mothers
sit clustered, suckling infants
half-concealed by embroidered capes;
a kid scows at his Gameboy; his canary-yellow t-shirt
shows an angry pencil bending to shout
I'm gonna wipe you out!
A laptop screen flits between Arabic and English
until a hand folds its flat wings together.
Huge Americans shout across the crowded prairie
of Samsonite cases, over-sharing more than words:
I'm looking forward to showering! one yells.
Can't hear a word you're saying, Carol! bellows another.

From this background I zoom in
on two women, who've created their own still space,
sitting to complete their evening prayers,
dipping veiled heads to the littered floor,
stretching fingertips towards the earth beneath it.
Behind them, a notice in several languages requests
'please use the masjid facilities for ablutions.'
The caption is illustrated by a simple diagram.
Outside, the sunset does its stuff without fuss.
The tannoy summons me, and I comply. ✎

II. Golden Horn

On the Bosphorus, a tug pulls
a silver slice of dawn light westwards,
dragging Asia towards Europe.
Overhead, a vapour trail scores the brightening sky:
the lines thread the coast of this landmass.
In Gülhane Park, there are gaudy bedding plants,
but something else perfumes the air.
Crows peck at the empty paths
beneath flocks of green parrots
which shimmer and scold in the canopy.
Pillars, walls, gates (locked and open)
stutter their fragments of history,
tales of empires fallen, hopes squandered,
lands plundered and re-appropriated.

Ayesophia is fenced off for repairs;
but still the vacant street behind it is watched
by sleepy guards in glassfronted cubes,
Republicans drafted to keep the truce
between pasts and presents. It's 6 a.m.
Trees lean over the brick enclosure.
A lone visitor stoops to scoop a handful
of flowers fallen below the back wall
of Justinian's purloined basilica,
crushes the fading petals,
inhales with their fragrance
the ghost of incense offered up
six hundred years ago. ⁄⁄

III. At Sultanahmet Mosque

A woman walking here needs a chaperone,
even at this early hour,
when only the sharpest salesman
has started to serve his gritty brew.
But in place of this, her sole companion
is a yellow dog. Its pace is slow.

Like a good Muslim wife,
it lags three paces behind,
and when the woman is lured
by the pungent aroma of coffee
it settles nearby, exhales heavily,
stretching nose over paws.

Sit, sit here. Let me dust it for you.
Here are my children in this picture.
Are you married?

Then the woman walks with the dog
in the white morning glow.
It sniffs at her pale, bare feet
and her trailing shawl. She dangles
her sandals from one hand.

It's hours yet till it opens,
so they honour the mosque
as best they can, criss-crossing
the courtyards, and circling
its blue-tinged walls. ⁄⁄

Credo

Chalcedon, Golden Horn. Anno Domini 451.
The Church Fathers are fed up;
their stiff robes chafe; their doctrines
don't sit comfortably, either.
Cyril's ghost wags a gnarled finger at Nestorius,
who's suffering from indigestion, even in the afterlife.
Spectres of Egyptian monks lay down their cudgels.

Unforgiving heat; unyielding diatribes;
the scribe flexes his cramped wrist.
An impartial slave flips the fan languidly.
His throat's so dry he cannot summon spit
to shift the fly climbing his thin, brown shin.
On palace roofs, bright-winged birds heckle.

A freeman clocks the whirring insect
with dispassion: he's in the wrong gathering,
but waits to see if there are seeds of Dharma
to be picked from this Christological squabble.
He flicks through a mental catalogue of sutra,
alights on the Metta-Sutta: *loving kindness.*

Long Preston, May time, round about now.
The sunrise cranks up an ambitious spread,
suggests its gentle warmth might raise the pearly haze.

A walker out for an early stroll observes
layers of green valleys unveiling themselves;
disturbs the midges crowning a cowpat
thinks – they've missed a bit, these holy men.

They've failed to grasp that some believe
that every day should offer glimpses
of hillsides, unfolding between meadows
and English attempts at cloudless skies.
They may not yearn for uncontested truths

shackling divine power with human rules,
but rather wait for rainfall's cleansing grace,
hope dry stone walls protect both sheep and man,
and know that birdsong heals. ⫽

Silence in Court

"Many years!" the courtiers acclaim
(loudest of all the one with a phial
of death-dealing venom up his sleeve),
"Many years to Basil, the great, the holy one!"
The engineer pockets his oily feather,
puffs out his cheeks in relief
as the jewelled lions stretch
their hinged jaws, bang on time
to roar their welcome
to the emperor, the elect one
who opened his eyes in the purple chamber,
swaddled in ritual, suckled with greatness.
The gilded cats thump their tasselled tails
on the smooth marble floor.
The procession begins.
    It's Constantinople, around a thousand AD.
The Great Palace is sacred space
because it pertains to the person
of a stocky man with a frivolous younger brother,
Basil the Macedonian, soldier, statesman –
latterly ascetic. Even the silence
in the splendid rooms is holy, protected by

DRING!

    It's Leeds, Festival time, 2013.
On the doorstep, home for a break,
a smiling demi-god in muddy jeans.
Many years I leaped into action
leaving my books to service these young heirs.
Long bath, hot food, clean clothes and he's off
before the Byzantine banquet begins.
    Silence is sacred, protected back then
by a pompous official in the pay of the court.
Soft-soled, obsequious he shuffles along
its echoing corridors, parched in the sun.
In my carpeted study, computer keys clack.

WEST

Epiphany

A bathroom's not a common place
for an epiphany, but there it was –
not holiness revealed, but hope.

No thunderclap or lightningbolt
on steep mountainside
where God withholds his face,

no whiff of sulphur, stagey drumroll
and swirling cloak
for the transformation scene,

just cranberry scented steam
beading the glass of chilled wine
poured by the same hands

that mixed hot and cold water,
splashed in the fragrant bubbles
and placed a towel within reach,

hospitable hands revealing
to this battered guest
tomorrow brightening the horizon.

Private Audience

The forest routes are marked
by blue or yellow arrows
though if you've wheels to manoeuver, best follow
the animal trail. Admire this heron,
who ducks his head into a woody breast.
Marvel at a pig-faced bat as big as a nightmare.

Unencumbered, I find my own path,
my cautious inner child stamping
and singing (in case of adders)
"we are his people, and the sheep,
and the sheep of his pasture."

In eight hours London will trip-switch itself
into Olympic mode.
Thousands of performers will gyrate
for millions of viewers glued to screens of every size,
behind them the windows open to the night air.

Fireworks will roar and splutter,
and crowds will cheer and chatter,
and later there will be medals and bouquets,
and ejaculations of champagne,

but none so blessed as I am,
honoured by a private audience with a damselfly.
She freedances with hot, still air
in a sundeep dingle,
bracken is wick with fleeting brown wings;
the only soundtrack
the streams' stereophonic chuckle. ✎

Cormorant

Almost all blackish, with a good deal of gloss,
favouring the Black and Caspian Seas
(also West Greenland and Sardinia).
Partial migrant in Europe, breeds
sometimes together with herons in high trees,
sometimes in reed beds. Nests
consisting of sticks, also seaweed.

There is a sharply demarcated white patch
on cheeks and chins (distinguishing them
from shags). Sexually mature
at three years, immatures
have whitish underparts; in summer
a white patch appears on the thighs.

Some have whitish underparts – both male
and female almost all blackish
(with a good deal of gloss).
Some have whitish heads.
A white patch appears on the thighs.

In summer, sometimes in reed beds
and sometimes in high trees
it winters in western and Mediterranean areas.

Single-brooded, breeds colonially, nests
with a finer lining (but sticks, also seaweed).
Predominantly fish, especially eels,
eels caught by diving while swimming
sometimes in reed beds and
sometimes in high trees.

Partial migrant, single-brooded, almost all blackish.

A sonorous 'chrochrochro' with manifold variations
as well as croaking and hissing noises may be heard

at the nest site, sharply demarcated
croaking and hissing
whitish parts may be found.

Seaweed sonorous, eels swimming. ⁄⁄

All in a Day's Work

As I unpack my week's supplies a ginger cat
swaggers through the back door; his proud tail
declares his status as permanent inhabitant.
He takes up residence on the sofa,
preferring, at meals times, one of the dining chairs.

The first evening I look up from my tapestry
and glimpse my landlord
striding past the window.
Beside him staggers a cow, unbalanced
by her newly emptied womb;
and that black bundle in his arms
must be her calf. Its spindly legs
flop limply below the man's elbow.

Next day as I descended from the viewpoint
with eyes still filled with the setting sun
I saw the famer busy in the barn;
we lean on the gate, chat about his herd,
and with a ready smile he warns
of *some commotion in the morning –*
the vet's coming at nine thirty, mind.
So after breakfast I boot up;
the coastal path entices me with seagulls,
upswirling spray, chilly gusts,
defiantly bright gorse under the fickle sky.

Mapless, hungry, I head inland, spot a familiar barn
and pause to inspect a metal pen, its articulated limbs
shining under sudden sunlight.
The dropped restraining straps slump in a chaotic pile
and smears of blood brighten the silver bars –
and here, half covered by black tufts,
the amputated testicles are formless as fallen fledglings,
their life-force glazing under a brisk wind.
Another lies separate from the rest,
a trophy, it seems, for the friendly feline
who calls, plaintively, from the cottage doorstep
for warmth and shelter. ⁄⁄

Time and Motion Study

Oh yes, bach, you can share my bench.
His eyes smiled brighter than his stained dentures,
and I lower my well-stretched body to its rest.

We discuss the price of milk and fishing quotas,
while I sip at fair trade Guatemalan coffee,
and he tells me he's lived here since
he swapped the blind red tides of his mother's womb
for the salt wave's crashing shingle
on the harbour front at Abercastle.

In the season it's mackerel and pollack.
And then, I ask, when they're gone?
*Crabs and that – and when there's little here
we go over Fishguard, see, but there
you have to watch the currents*
which he shapes with his hands.
*There's two that come together, moving fast,
and you've only five minutes to fetch
twenty lobster pots in before – you know –*

And I wonder what alchemy of ear and eye
showed him how to catch that moment,
I, who cannot tell a chough from a crow
without a book.

After dinner, I put my boots back on,
to climb inside the fort at Garn Fawr,
and turn to watch the sea's insatiable maw
swallow the last of the sunlight. ⁄⁄

Land Ahoy

Was it mid-day when you landed?
Burly men gripped your aching limbs
as you splashed into the shallows,
and there was bunting, and cheering,
and your hand was pumped
by every man-jack of the crowd.
There was a brass-band playing
'Land of our Fathers', and gnats' piss beer
in pewter tankards, served from a barrel
brought down from the Trefin hotel,
with a buxom girl twisting the brass tap
in red, raw fingers, and dogs barking,
and snot-snouted lads shoving each other:
'take a message to the telegraph office, mister?
The pony and trap's waiting.'

Or was it dawn, with no reception
but retired Ableseaman Billy Pritchard?
He was watching the tide fill up the harbour,
tamping down his first pipe of the day
and shifting his peg-leg off the bench.
He raised his tweed cap to you, and asked:
'Is it good crabs, where you come from, then?'
And all you wanted was to be still,
to no longer feel the deck ducking and diving,
to hear the waves slapping the shingle,
to see something that wasn't sea-blue
or mist-grey or cloud-white –
that burst of gorse on the cliff,
the flags of ragged robin fluttering in the hedge,
even the yellow spirals of a landsnail's shell.

Molly Lamb

The lighthouse strobe pierces the darkness,
skimming brightness round the edge of a barn,
fanning its rhythm through uncurtained windows.
Below it, the short beam of the farmer's torch
lumbers across a field; halts for a while.
He carries the last bottle of the day
to the Molly lamb sleeping in an old hen hut –
the fox got the lot of them:
nothing but feathers there was in the morning,
he tells me. And by daylight
the two-day orphan looks pale and flighty
as feathers, pointless as a bag of rubbish.

But he levers up onto his knees
as I approach, rump inelegantly raised
in that awkward way sheep have,
tremulous in the brisk sea breezes
that claw over the windbreak.
His eyes have the dark expressionlessness
of all newborn mammals. I offer
the teat of a plastic bottle
patterned with bright monkeys;
he grips and sucks, drains it in seconds.
I have no idea whether he leans
his bony cheek against my leg
out of fatigue or sentiment;
the farmer and I are all the mothering
he's known, but it barely comforts him,
and he folds himself back down onto the straw.

Within days, he's firmer on his legs,
though such puny pipecleaner limbs
are laughable contenders for rams' shoulders.
The farmer brings me extra firewood
by way of thanks; the wind's got up,
roars down my chimney
to rouse the embers. Later, I go outside

to watch this day's extravagant experiment
with the same old elements of light and air,
a thousand permutations of perfection
as if the Almighty were undecided
which proof of omnipotence to patent.

I listen to the night sounds, thinking about
the voided fields after foot and mouth's holocaust,
the trucks of yearlings hastening to market,
all the unpalatable economics of livestock farming.
But morning sees me crouched again
beside his pen, stroking the thin curls
as he butts me, coaxing him outside
so he can get the sun on his back. ⁄⁄

Ophelia at Llanwnda

There's plenty of water here for drowning sorrows,
hastening down clefts in the cliff,
dawdling below the pebbles
on the beach at Abermawr.
Trail your fingers into it; anoint your face,
lave the crazed pieces of your mind.
If you want a coronet, there's an armful of choice
from flowers that have other tasks
than forming your funeral tribute:
violets are breakfast for the bumble bee
who bludgeons between their pursed lips.
Meadowsweet's red staff inching through ivy
stores up slow-release fragrance.
Celandines smile at passing feet
and gorse holds aloft beacons for the sunshine.
The roll-call in the hedgerow's wholesome:
Wound-wort, Self-heal. //

Last Invasion

On the twenty-second of February, 1797,
French soldiers stumbled off the boat in Cwm Felin,
stomachs heaving from the voyage
and wine plundered from a shipwreck.
They forced their way through ivy tendrils
and frosted thornbushes, set up camp at Carreg Wastad.
At nightfall, they wrapped themselves in dank coats,
their Gallic lice playing host to local creepie-crawlies.

A tapestry dresses them in bright uniforms;
shame is stitched into their faces,
showing how they were tricked to surrender
by swirling russet shawls: no manly foe,
but one Jemima Nicholas, huge-bosomed Celtic matron,
who used only peasant tools
to mislead an invading army
too wasted to recognize petticoats.

A bay or two south, each Easter holidays,
English tourists emerge from a people carrier.
Kids rehoist a swing from the tree,
jolly rogers, planning high jinks for the week.
Mum unpacks organic goodies from the coolbox;
Dad fiddles with the barbeque, pours
a restorative glass of merlot.
At night, they check how many more pieces
are missing from the jigsaw they do
when the sea's too rough for wetsuits.

Up on the headland, indigenous vixen
turns her head at my approach.
The cub curled below her jaw rocks for a moment,
then, in a tawny flash, they go to ground in the gorse.
Sunlight hangs the shadow of a gull
on the rough drapery of the cliff.
To them all, and the small brown butterflies,
I bow my head in homage,
honouring true sovereignty. //

Tyddewi Revisted

Someone had just left in a hurry –
God himself, I think – leaving ugly seats
leaning against the slanting purple slate.
I imagine him levering himself
out of the Bishop's throne
and striding down the nave,
brandishing his crook above his head
and roaring imprecations in Welsh
at oblivious pairs of lambs,
all flashing eyes and swirling whiskers
like an arthritic bard, declaiming
'I'm coming home!' as he stumbles
on the footpath to the chapel
rooted on the cliff.
'Leave the door open!' he shouts,
'so the seagull's cry can perch on the altar stones
and the children's prayers float onto the crest of the wave,
and let the chairs stand ready
for a weary walker to rest a while
especially if she can't find the right words
in either language to call me by my name.'
And he swoops off into the sea-mist,
the hem of his robe towed by a kittiwake.

Hannah Stone

Hannah Stone was born in London and has lived in Leeds for over twenty five years. She has recently completed an MA in Creative Writing at Leeds Trinity University, for which she established the Imprint *Wordspace* currently published by Indigo Dreams Publishing. *Perfect Timing* was published on Createspace as an assignment for the MA in 2014. Since then her work has been published in anthologies, journals and online platforms, most recently with Gill Lambert and Maria Preston in *An After Dinner's Sleep*, ed. Oz Hardwick (Indigo Dreams Publishing, Beaworthy, 2015) and in *New Crops from Old Fields: Eight Medievalist Poets*, ed. Oz Hardwick (Stairwell Books, York, 2015). She was awarded the Yorkshire Prize in the Poetry Business Book and Pamphlet Competition, 2014-5. *Lodestone* is her first solo collection. Hannah is well known on the Yorkshire spoken word circuit, has contributed to an arts festival in Murcia, Spain and is due to read in Boston, Mass. She participated in the Leeds Lieder project in 2015-16, collaborating with Leeds College of Music composer Howard Auster. Her work responds to libraries, art, landscapes, contemporary and historical political situations and to the beguiling puzzle which is humanity.

Other anthologies and collections available from Stairwell Books

For further information please contact rose@stairwellbooks.com

www.stairwellbooks.co.uk
@stairwellbooks

VICTOR HUGO

EXPLORES

GUERNSEY

GREGORY STEVENS COX

in collaboration with Stephen Foote

**BLUE
ORMER**

MMXIX

Respectueusement dédié à

Hélène Waysbord

Copyright © 2019 Gregory Stevens Cox & Stephen Foote.

ISBN 978-1-9998913-6-7

Published by Blue Ormer Publishing, 2019.

www.blueormer.co.uk

Book layout and cover design by Stephen Foote.

Cover image: Victor Hugo, *Plainmont, la maison visionée*
Bibliothèque nationale de France.

Printed in Guernsey by Printed.gg.

CONTENTS

HOW TO USE THIS BOOK:

This book describes five excursions. They were designed in the Victorian era for carriage drives and each excursion was planned to take one day. That allowed plenty of time for a leisurely enjoyment of locations and the opportunity to walk and lunch. Hugo regularly condensed his carriage tours into two hours. That was sufficient time to cover excursions one and two; and sufficient to cover much of excursions three, four, and five. The modern tourist can adopt the swift or slow approach.

Literary pilgrims exploring the country of *The Toilers of the Sea* should undertake excursions two and five. Those who are interested in Hugo's life are advised to consider excursions one and three. Excursion four works happily with either schedule.

A 'Hugo holiday' in Guernsey would ideally last a week – two days to roam around Hugo's St Peter Port (for which see *Victor Hugo's St Peter Port*, Blue Ormer, 2018) and five days to devote to the excursions described in this book.

Each excursion in this book is accompanied by the relevant section of a contemporary map – published by Stephen Barbet in 1869. This accurately represents Hugo's Guernsey. The road system was much the same then as now but it should be noted that the coastal road at Vale Castle did not exist in Hugo's day, St Julian's Avenue was opened in 1873 and the Val des Terres road dates from the 1930s.

FORESAY

People regularly think of Victor Hugo and Hauteville House, almost as though he lived as a recluse or prisoner in his house. In this monograph I hope to demonstrate that Hugo explored Guernsey thoroughly and enjoyed touring it. In the years 1856–1864 he walked, particularly on the east and south coasts. In the years 1865–1870 he enthusiastically went on carriage excursions, making 350 expeditions into the country parishes. He knew the island far better than most of its inhabitants.

Hugo incorporated exquisite descriptions of the island in his novel *The Toilers of the Sea*. So this monograph aims to serve as a *vade mecum* for literary pilgrims wishing to follow in the steps of Gilliatt. The monograph also seeks to describe the importance of the island in Hugo's daily life. Guernsey was home to Hugo. There were locations that he loved, views that captivated him. Bathing at Fermain, taking picnics at Moulin Huet, visiting friends on the west coast, inspecting the animal market at the Castel, examining prehistoric monuments, campaigning to preserve Vale Castle – these were just some of his activities. Guernsey was both Hugo's home and a literary inspiration. We should think of Hugo and Guernsey just as we couple Hardy and Dorset, the Brontës and Yorkshire, Scott and Scotland.

Guernsey today is not precisely the Guernsey that Hugo knew. We have composed this book around extracts from a contemporary guidebook – *THE CHANNEL ISLANDS: A Guide to Jersey, Guernsey, Sark, Herm, Jethou, Alderney, Etc.* by Frank Fether Dally, published by Edward Stanford, London, 1860. This was a guide designed for 'Visitors and Residents. With Notes on Their History, Geology, Climate, Health and Disease, Farming, Gardening, Indigenous Vegetation, and Laws.' Dally's guide presents Guernsey as Hugo's contemporaries knew and understood it. Hugo's writings about Guernsey history and antiquities should be read in the context of the contemporary understanding of these matters.

The text is complemented by engravings, photographs, watercolours, and sketches which illustrate Victorian Guernsey. There are also some modern photographs which portray the timeless geography of the island.

Gregory Stevens Cox
April 2019

ABBREVIATIONS

Agenda	the notebooks kept by Hugo 1855–1870; to be found in Massin (see M below).
Chenay	Chenay, Paul *Victor Hugo à Guernesey, souvenirs inédits de son beau-frère* Paris 1902.
Cox *Neighbours*	Cox, Gregory *Victor Hugo's Guernsey Neighbours* Guernsey 2016.
Cox *Perspectives*	Cox, Gregory *Les Travailleurs de la mer – some Guernsey perspectives* Guernsey 2016.
Dally	Dally, Frank *The Channel Islands: A Guide to Jersey, Guernsey, Sark, Herm, Jethou, Alderney, Etc.* 1860.
de Havilland	de Havilland, Mrs James *Recollections of Victor Hugo* Guernsey [1909].
Kendrick	Kendrick, Thomas *The Archaeology of the Channel Islands. Volume 1: The Bailiwick of Guernsey* London 1928.
L'Archipel	Hugo, Victor *L'Archipel de la Manche* (M xii/514-546).
M	Massin's edition of the works of Hugo – *Œuvres complètes de Victor Hugo: édition chronologique* Club Français du Livre, 1967-1970. – 18 volumes. M xiv/1400 = Massin, volume 14, page 1400.
Toilers	Hugo, Victor *Toilers of the Sea*. The novel is divided into parts, books, chapters. *Toilers* I/i/3 = Part one, book one, chapter 3. The translations used in the monograph are taken from the first English translation. *Les Travailleurs de la mer* (*The Toilers of the Sea*) was first published in 1866.

6

ᛁNTRODUCTION

It is an innocent and enjoyable pastime to follow in the footsteps of Gilliatt, the hero of *The Toilers of the Sea*. Following the publication of the English translation in 1866, literary pilgrims ventured across the Channel to view the haunted house at Pleinmont. Guidebooks of the Victorian and Edwardian eras helped them on their quest. More recently the French have travelled to the island, a copy of Gérard Pouchain's *Promenades dans l'archipel de la Manche avec un guide nommé Victor Hugo* tucked under the arm.

At one level this book is intended to serve as such a guide. Hugo had a remarkable ability to describe buildings and landscapes with precision. Who can forget his characterisation of Torteval church –

> Three o'clock had sounded in the steeple of Torteval which is round and pointed like a magician's hat. [*Toilers* I/v/5].

Perhaps obvious – but for most of us only after Hugo has told us.

To follow Hugo around Guernsey is a privilege – his poetic vision enhances our mundane observation. This book has, however, a deeper purpose. Hugo had an extensive knowledge about Guernsey. He was interested in its geology, geography, natural history, antiquities, history, patois, traditions, and folklore. Hugo intertwined these themes in his fiction. Further, Hugo developed a genuine affection for the island. Hugo needs to be understood in his Guernsey context.

Following his arrival in 1855 Hugo was consciously an exile and pined for his native France [see pp.9-10 below]. But in due course he came to appreciate Guernsey. This reached its climax when he dedicated *The Toilers of the Sea* to the island of Guernsey and its people –

Je dédie ce livre
au rocher d'hospitalité et de liberté,
à ce coin de vieille terre normande
où vit le noble petit peuple de la mer,
à l'île de Guernesey, sévère et douce,
mon asile actuel, mon tombeau probable.

V.H.

[*I dedicate this book to the rock of hospitality and liberty,*
to that portion of old Norman ground, inhabited by the
noble little nation of the sea, to the Island of Guernsey,
severe yet kind, my present asylum, perhaps my tomb. V.H.]

This dedication deserves attention. 'My present asylum...' – we know that Hugo returned to France in 1870. But we know that with the benefit of hindsight. Writing in 1865 Hugo had good reason to believe that he might never again set foot in France. Exile was painful to him. 'Perhaps my tomb' – Hugo had reached an age when death was not too far distant. We know that he lived into his eighties – but that again is with the benefit of hindsight. An exile, contemplating his death. Death was ever present for Hugo in 1864–5. Emilie de Putron, the fiancée of Hugo's son François-Victor, was dying. She explained to Hugo that she did not want to die. She wrote eloquently about death shortly before her last day and Hugo received her notes. He incorporated some of her thoughts in the moving funeral oration that he delivered at the Foulon cemetery [Cox *Perspectives* pp.62-3].

Exile and Death were themes central to Hugo when writing *The Toilers of the Sea*. Gilliatt, of French origin and living in Guernsey, makes a night journey over the sea and then a descent into the abyss. Gilliatt survives mortal combat with the octopus and returns to Guernsey. His ordeal has changed him. He accepts the loss of his beloved Déruchette, he helps her to marry the man she loves, he organises their departure. Altruistic and accepting, he surrenders to Nature, the sea takes him. The descent of Gilliatt into the abyss is in a high literary tradition – the descent into Hades of Odysseus, the descent of Dante into the Inferno.

We remember that Hugo originally intended to call his novel *l'Abîme*.

Jung and his school drew on Homer and the literary tradition to employ the images of the Nekyia (the night journey on the sea and descent to hell) and of Katabasis (descent into the lower world) as metaphors for a descent into the dark depths of the unconscious ... a journey to hell and death. I suggest that the Nekyia and Katabasis of Gilliatt mirror a psychological journey made by Hugo in 1864–5. By writing, and in writing, *The Toilers of the Sea* Hugo grappled with inner conflicts and anxieties. Like his creation Gilliatt, he came to accept Nature and the relationship of man and Nature. In traversing Hugo's Guernsey we should remember not just the adventures of Gilliatt but also the journeys, physical and spiritual, of Hugo.

1855–1865 WALKING AND EXPLORATION

In the first decade of his exile Hugo energetically explored Guernsey. These were years of observation and learning. The culmination of Hugo's efforts came to a flowering with the writing of *The Toilers of the Sea* and its Introduction. During this decade Hugo walked a lot. He described Gilliatt walking in the following terms –

> ...he had had a peculiar manner of traversing the country in all parts without being observed. He knew the bye-paths, and favoured solitary and winding routes; he had the shy habits of a wild beast who knows that he is disliked, and keeps at a distance. [M III/iii/5].

Hugo perhaps walked in that fashion in the early days of exile. Writing in 1865 he described himself in the third person –

> Ten or twelve years ago a Frenchman who had only recently arrived in Guernsey was roaming along one of the western beaches, lonely, sad, bitter, thinking of his lost country. In Paris you stroll (*on flâne*), in Guernsey you roam (*on rôde*). It seemed to him that this island was a gloomy place. The fog

covered everything, the shore resounded under the breakers, the seas pounded huge sheets of spray off the rocks, the sky was menacing and black. Yet it was Spring; but the sea's Spring has a savage name. It is called the Equinox. It is more readily a hurricane than a breeze; and it's worth recording that one day in May the spray, fanned by this wind, leaped twenty feet above the top of the signal-mast on the highest platform of Castle Cornet. This Frenchman felt that he must be in England; he did not know a word of English; he could see an old Union Jack, torn by the wind, flying over a ruined tower at the end of a deserted promontory; there were two or three cottages there; in the distance, all was sand, heather, moorland, spiky gorse; a few low-built artillery barracks, with wide embrasures, their corners showing; the stones hewn by man looked as sad as the rocks worked by the sea; the Frenchman could feel in himself that thickening of anguish which is the beginning of nostalgia; he looked, he listened; not a ray of light; cormorants hunting, skudding clouds; all along the horizon a leaden heaviness; a huge pale curtain falling from the zenith; the ghost of melancholy in the shroud of tempests; not a thing anywhere which promised hope, and nothing to remind him of his country; this Frenchman was musing, getting more and more depressed; suddenly he lifted his head; a voice was coming from one of the cottage, the door half-open, a clear, fresh, delicate voice, a child's voice, and this voice was singing

La clef des champs, la clef des bois
La clef des amourettes! [M xii/536]

[*Free to roam the fields, Free to roam the woods,*
Free for flirtations!]

The joyful sound of a Guernsey child singing medieval French lifted Hugo's soul. The song is the very spirit of his poetry collection *les Chansons des rues et des bois* published in 1865.

Hugo's brother-in-law Paul Chenay described him speeding up hill and down dale, causing Chenay some difficulty in keeping up. Hugo revealed his discoveries, regaling his guest with historical facts and local traditions; the guest was proud to constitute the audience of one. They visited sites on the south coast [see page 131]; and on a moonlit night they walked to the Vale to explore the prehistoric monuments [see page 69].

Nature flourished luxuriantly in Guernsey and Hugo appreciated it. He jotted comments in his notebooks about the first swallow and the first cuckoo of spring. He appreciated flowers and insects and wrote fondly about them.

> The grass in Guernsey is ordinary grass – however it is a little richer; a meadow in Guernsey is very much like a lawn at Cuges or Gémenos. As in any grass, it contains fescues and meadow-grasses; but there is also brome-grass with spindle-like spikelets, canary-grass, the agrostis which produces a green dye, rye-grass, yorkshire fog with wool on its stems, sweet-smelling vernal grass, quaking-grass, flute-grass, cat's flote tail grass, foxtails with spikes like little clubs, feather-grass whose stems can be used to make baskets, sand-binding lyme-grass. And that is not all. There is also cock's foot, whose flowers are closely clustered together, millet-grass and even – according to some local agronomists – andropogon... Now imagine a thousand insects making their way through the grass or flying over it, some of them hideous, others delightful; under the grass, beetles with long antennae and long proboscises, calandra weevils, ants milking aphids – their cows – slobbering grasshoppers, ladybirds, which are God's creatures, click-beetles, which belong to the devil; on the grasses and in the air, dragon-flies, ichneumon-flies, wasps, rose-beetles, velvety bumble-bees, gauzy lace-wings, red-bellied ruby-tails, noisy syrphid flies. Then you will have some idea of the fanciful display to be seen in June at midday on Jerbourg Ridge or in Fermain Bay by an entomologist

who is something of a dreamer and a poet who is something of a naturalist. [M xii/517-8].

'A poet who is something of a naturalist...' – Hugo managed to combine the rôles successfully. His sensitive vignette of a bucolic scene is reminiscent of Vergil's *Georgics* –

> In the evening, the radiantly horizontal setting sun sheds its light into the sunken roads and onto the heifers slowly returning home, lingering to nibble at the hedges on either side; this makes the dogs bark. [M xii/521].

Hugo's keen eye was not reserved solely for nature. He noted architectural details –

> A stone hut on a road at Les Hubits has on the corner of a wall a stump of a pillar with a date, 1405. [M xii/520].

Hugo studied the island and its people in a helpful environment. In the mid-19th century Guernsey was home to some scholars who were actively investigating the geology, archaeology, history, folklore, and natural history of the island. Frederick **Lukis** and his children made important archaeological discoveries both in Guernsey and abroad. Frederick became a member of the Society of Antiquaries of London in 1853. His son, the Rev. William Collings Lukis, was a regular contributor to the journals of the British Archaeological Association and other learned societies. Typical of his research was the essay 'Danish Cromlechs and Burial Customs compared with those of Brittany, the Channel Islands, and Great Britain' published in the *Wiltshire Archaeological and Natural History Magazine* (8, 1864, pp. 145–69). The *opus magnum* of Ferdinand Brock **Tupper** – *The History of Guernsey and its Bailiwick; with occasional notices of Jersey* – was published in 1854, shortly before Hugo's arrival in Guernsey. The poet George **Métivier** was hard at work on his patois dictionary during the 1860s. In 1862 he was visited by Prince Louis-Lucien Bonaparte and translated the Gospel according to Matthew into Guernésiais for publication by the prince. Professor David **Ansted**, Fellow of the Royal Society, lived for a while in Guernsey in the 1860s. He occasionally lectured and was co-author with Robert Gordon Latham of *The Channel Islands* (1862). How we see the world and understand it, together with the link between art and science, were themes developed by Ansted in his lectures (see *The Art Journal*, 1864, volume 10, page 84). Ansted enhanced his book with paintings by Paul Jacob **Naftel**, an islander who painted scores of water-colour studies of local scenes. Foreign artists were attracted to Guernsey. Sarah Louisa **Kilpack** visited the Channel Islands in the 1850s and 1860s. She enjoyed painting maritime scenes, particularly rocky coastal landscapes. Her images of diminutive figures juxtaposed to the stormy sea echo some of Hugo's perceptions. At the same time the camera was challenging artists and writers.

The fruits of research found their way into local guide books such as Frank Fether Dally's THE CHANNEL ISLANDS: *A Guide to Jersey, Guernsey, Sark, Herm, Jethou, Alderney, Etc* (1860) *designed For Visitors and Residents. With Notes on Their History, Geology, Climate, Health and Disease, Farming, Gardening, Indigenous Vegetation, and Laws.* For example, when dealing with prehistoric monuments Dally cited the essay by F.C. Lukis 'Observations on the Celtic Megaliths, and the contents of Celtic Tombs, chiefly as they remain in the Channel Islands' (*Archaeologia* volume 35, Issue 2 1854, pp. 232–258). We make considerable use of Dally's guidebook in this present monograph. It is of importance because it represents the general understanding of Guernsey at precisely the time that Hugo was exploring the island. What Dally wrote was known to educated islanders, to the carriage drivers, and to the editors of Guernsey newspapers, the very people with whom Hugo mixed.

From the summer of 1864 until the spring of 1865 Hugo was busy writing *The Toilers of the Sea*. His topographical descriptions demonstrate an excellent knowledge of the north-east coast, from St Peter Port to L'Ancresse; and the south coast – *le Port au quatrième étage, le Gouffre, la Maison hantée, le Moulin Huet, Roquaine-Baie, Pleinmont. The Toilers of the Sea* is set in the 1820s, the narrator belongs to the 1860s. The novel consequently enjoys two time perspectives. The reader is made aware of Guernsey in the 1820s and the 1860s. This admits of historical meditations with contrasts between 'then' and 'now.' In describing locations such as St Sampson's, Hugo is able to contrast the old village of the 1820s with the busy harbour town that he knew.

During the years 1855–1864 we occasionally find Hugo travelling by 'cab' or phaeton. A 'Norton cab' was a vehicle hired from George Norton in St John Street or Joseph Norton in College Street, St Peter Port. A phaeton could be hired from Read's near Ann's Place (later at Cemetery Lane). A phaeton was an open carriage drawn by one or two horses. It had a lightly sprung body and four large wheels and could travel swiftly [M x/1399; *Barbet's Almanach* 1859]. Hugo's routine changed dramatically in 1865. If 1855–1864 was a decade of walking, 1865–1870 was a quinquennial of carriage drives. And if we see 1855–1864 as a time of exploring Guernsey, the years 1865–1870 can be characterised as years of enjoying the island.

HUGO'S CARRIAGE DRIVES 1865–1870

Soon after completing *The Toilers of the Sea* Hugo embarked on a series of carriage drives. Between 1 May and 26 June 1865 he went on 41 promenades. We are probably justified in linking these excursions to his writing *L'Archipel de la Manche*. Hugo composed this in 1865 and submitted the text to the publishers of *les Travailleurs de la mer* but it was not until 1883 that it was printed.

Hugo clearly enjoyed his excursions and they became a regular feature of his annual calendar. In spring and summer every year – prior to his Continental holiday – he went for carriage drives in the afternoon. He was usually accompanied by Juliette Drouet. The number was often made up to four by the inclusion of his sister-in-law and a servant. Sometimes Sénat the dog was taken along. The excursions usually lasted two hours and the standard fee was 3 fr 60. Almost all of the *promenades* were *en calèche* – an elegant four-wheeled carriage with a folding top (see photo on page 30). On a few occasions, when his family was visiting, Hugo hired a larger *voiture*.

1865	41 *promenades*	1 May – 26 June
1866	44 *promenades*	5 April – 10 June; holiday; 24 October – 2 November
1867	72 *promenades*	29 March – 13 July
1868	64 *promenades*	9 May – 24 July
1869	82 *promenades*	12 April – 28 July [no 18 bis]
1870	47 *promenades*	20 April – 10 July
TOTAL	350	

Hugo recorded the itineraries in 1868–1870. It is possible to distinguish five route patterns. These correspond quite closely with the routes described in contemporary guidebooks:

South-East – Fermain, St Martin's (Dally, Excursion 1)
North-East – St Sampson's, Vale (Dally, Excursion 2)
West Coast – Cobo (Dally, Excursion 3)
West Coast – Rocquaine, St Saviour's (Dally, Excursion 4)
South Coast – Pleinmont (Dally, Excursion 5)

Hugo often followed precisely the route described by Dally. Sometimes he introduced variations – to visit friends or to view a locality that held a particular importance for him. Hugo did not always make a full guidebook excursion. For example, he sometimes followed Dally's Second Excursion as far as St Sampson's, no further. On other days he went further, to L'Ancresse and Vale Church.

The practicalities of roads and lanes played a determining role. The *calèche* proceeded at the pace of the horses walking. Taking into consideration the nature of the Guernsey terrain, the average speed was probably about 5 mph. Hugo's *promenades* lasted for two hours. This meant that his excursions required a terminus not much further than 5 miles from Hauteville House. The guidebooks envisaged tourists spending a day on each excursion; as Hugo's outings lasted two hours he did not have the time available to complete in full Dally 3, 4 and 5. However, he made forays into those areas and over the course of his excursions he covered the ground described by Dally.

We catch glimpses of Hugo's excursions from reminiscences of his drivers. Peter Luscombe explained that Victor Hugo was wont to lean in the cab, silently meditating as the vehicle moved along. Suddenly, he would exclaim, '*Arrêtez, Monsieur Pierre!*' and then would hastily scribble the thoughts which had occurred to him.

Another carriage driver was Charles Shepherd. When interviewed by the *Guernsey Press* in 1937 he recollected –

> The poet had ladies with him, but said very little, being apparently deep in reverie. But, arrived at the Haunted House, he handed Mr Shepherd two francs as a pourboire… Once, when going down the zig-zag at Petit Bôt, Mr Shepherd spoke of his ch'va (horse). The poet replied in correction, "*Cheval,*' et quand tu parles de plus qu'un cheval, 'chevaux.*"* [https://www.priaulxlibrary.co.uk/articles/article/victor-hugo-and-guernsey-victor-hugos-coachmen]

According to Shepherd, Hugo's favourite drive was to the Haunted House, returning to Town via Rocquaine, Perelle, Grands Moulins and up the Talbot Valley. An analysis of the itineraries for 1868-1870 suggests that excursions to the Vale and to Cobo were much more frequent than to the Haunted House at Pleinmont. But Shepherd may be recollecting journeys of earlier years.

The five chapters that follow present excursions taking the Hugo pilgrim to all the parishes of the island. Each chapter consists of four sections –

1. A section map reproduced from Stephen Barbet's map of Guernsey published in 1869. (Route marked in red).
2. The text of Dally's excursion. This gives us an understanding

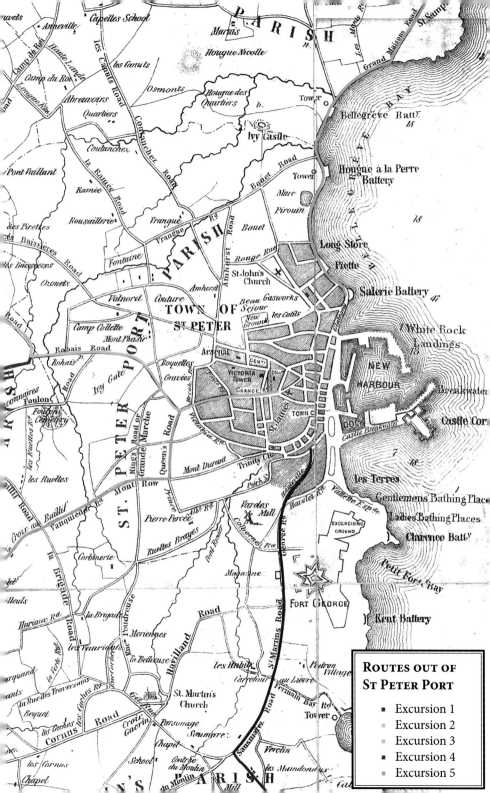

of the island as it was in Hugo's day.

3.   Images illustrative of locations mentioned by Dally. These have been drawn mainly from Victorian sources.

4.   Commentary by Gregory Stevens Cox, discussing the Hugo links of the area.

Departures and returns

The map on page 17 indicates the beginning of each of the Dally excursions. Hugo recorded little about his departure on carriage excursions. His itinerary notes for his return are more interesting. He often recorded his route home from the west as *Bailiff's Cross – Mount Row – Cosette Place – Pierre Percée*. There are two points of interest. First, Hugo studiously eschewed the new English road name *Prince Albert Road*; he used the traditional name *Pierre Percée*. The francophone republican had no time for English road names celebrating the British monarchy.

Secondly, we note *Cosette Place* – a location named by Hugo after a character in *les Misérables*. What and where was Cosette Place? On one occasion Hugo recorded his route out of town as *Petit Marché – Cosette Place – Mount Row*. This provides a complementary co-ordinate:-

Departure: ...*Petit Marché – Cosette Place – Mount Row*...
Return: ... *Mount Row – Cosette Place – Pierre Percée*...

Petit Marché was the traditional Guernsey name for Queen's Road, the new name displayed on Barbet's Guernsey map (see page 17). Cosette Place was at the intersection of four roads – Queen's Road, Mount Durand, Prince Albert Road, Mount Row in today's terms. Hard by this crossroads is Colborne Place. Steve Foote felicitously suggests that Hugo renamed **Colborne Place**, rejecting a British official (**Colborne**) in favour of **Co**sette. Moreover, Government House opposite, with its grounds, lawns, and trees, perhaps evoked Petit-Picpus and its grounds in *les Misérables*, the home of Cosette for several years.

Colborne Place – a Regency house proudly proclaiming its name on high –
was regularly called Cosette Place by Hugo (photo: Graham Jackson).

What is of considerable interest is that Hugo consciously linked the
Guernsey landscape to his fictional work – just as he viewed north-east
Guernsey as *le pays de Gilliatt.*

Hugo rode and meditated, he walked and meditated. As Baudelaire
wrote in 1868, gazing from France at Hugo in Guernsey:

> ...aujourd'hui il marche dans des solitudes peuplées par
> sa pensée. Ainsi est-il peut-être encore plus grand et plus
> singulier...toujours il nous apparaît comme la statue de la
> Méditation qui marche. [Baudelaire *L'art romantique*, Paris
> edition 1925 p.301.]
>
> [... *today he walks in solitudes populated by his thought. So he*
> *is, maybe, yet greater and odder...ever he seems to us to be the*
> *statue of Meditation that walks.*]

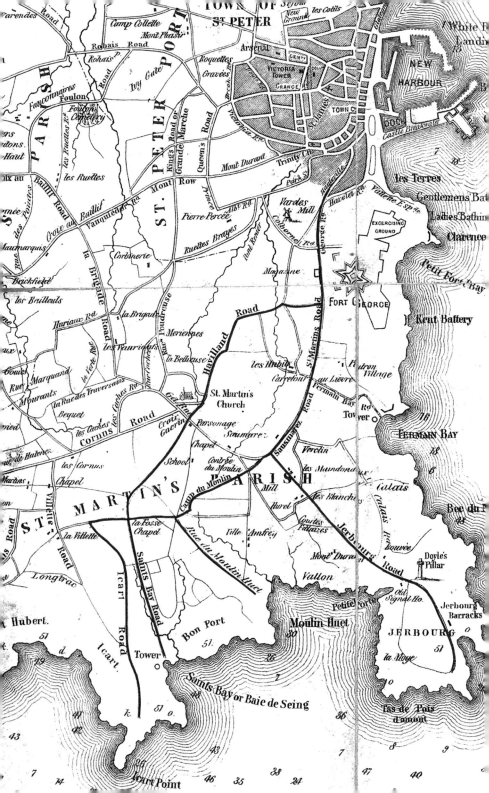

I: SOUTH EAST

EXCURSION 1

The Bays—Fermain Bay—Bec du Nez—Doyle Column—
Military Roads—Saumarez Manor-house—Jerbourg—Moulin
Houet Bay—Saint's Bay—Icart Point—St. Martin's Church—
Various return Routes.

In conducting the visitor through the island, the rides, drives, and
rambles will be arranged in distinct daily excursions. The tours may,
of course, be varied according to taste or convenience, by scanning
the description of each ; and plain directions are given for finding
the road to various parts.

The Bays

But few of the bays can be closely or advantageously approached
by a carriage. The drivers of hired vehicles know the locality of each,
and will convey visitors, who employ them, to the most available
spots for making the descent on foot, and wait their return, or
otherwise. In fact, it is the pedestrian alone who can fully realize the
charm of these scenes, both in approaching them, and in the changes
they unfold, as their grandeur suddenly or gradually develops itself
in successive contrasts. It is in the by-paths, in the retired and rural
lanes, that the lovers of nature will best appreciate the attractions
of these islands. Some of them, especially those leading to the bays,
are watered by a tiny rivulet, bubbling sweet music to the ear, and
fringed with ferns of exquisite and almost gigantic form. In other
lanes, the banks of the hedges are entirely formed of stones, on

21

the summit of which grows the furze, with its biennial bunches of golden flowers, and from every crevice peep forth the stonecrop, the penny-wort, and the graceful foxglove, the herb Robert, the dog violet, and multitudes of others ; while the stones themselves are treasures for a studio, prodigal of lichens, tinted with the varied hues of pale grey and green, rich orange, white and gold.

Fermain Bay

is the nearest to the town, and may be reached from the south esplanade by ascending the hill, passing the artillery barracks to the fort, and thence by a pathway along the edge of the cliffs. The usual road, either by Hautville and George Road, or by the carriage route to Fort George, has been already pointed out. Proceeding on the road to St. Martin's, about a mile from the town, is Fermain Lane, which descends to the bay through a steep but extremely beautiful glen, down the sides of which the road winds in a serpentine direction ; but so rough and narrow, as to be scarcely passable by a carriage. A small rivulet meanders through the middle of this glen, and passes invisibly to the sea. The line of the water's edge is nearly straight from one end of the bay to the other. At each side the waves contend with rugged and perpendicular walls of rock, against which their force seems expended in vain. The bay is protected on either side by a ledge of broken rocks, extending to a considerable distance into the sea, and breaking the force of the tumultuous waters, which often rage between it and the opposite coast of Sark. The lower part of the shore consists of a fine white sand, which gives a peculiar transparency to the waters, and above this the beach is formed of rounded pebbles. It is an excellent spot for ball-practice by the troops. A martello tower, on the heights above, defends the bay. The white tower points out to mariners a dangerous cluster of rocks, called The "Lower Heads," lying midway between this point and Sark.

The pedestrian should now take the pathway cut along the side of the cliff to his right, which conducts to a rocky headland, whence an extensive view is obtained of the eastern shore and the opposite islands. He will thus arrive at a small creek, where is an anchorage for a few fishing-boats, called the harbour of *Bec du Nez*. He may then proceed inland up a deep ravine, or wind his way by tortuous paths along the whole of this coast, till he reach the prominent object called

Doyle's Column.

The main road to this monument is by continuing on the road to St. Martin's, as far as an avenue of trees, where on the right hand stands *Saumarez Manor-house*. It has rather an imposing effect, with its handsome gateway and armorial bearings, but is let to a farmer with the adjoining land, and is sadly dilapidated. This is a very ancient fief, and has been in the possession of the De Saumarez family from time immemorial. One of its feudal privileges was, that if the *seigneur* wished to cross over to Jersey, his tenants were obliged to convey him thither once a year, on receiving three sols in money and their dinner.

Passing this estate, and leaving the road to the right, which leads to St. Martin's village, you reach the noble column erected by the States of Guernsey as a memorial of the public services of General Sir John Doyle, while lieutenant-governor of the island. We have elsewhere shown the success which attended the efforts of Sir John in rescuing from the sea a large track of land at the Vale at the expense of Government ; added to this, on the renewal of hostilities with France, in 1803, he proceeded with zeal and perseverance to place the island in a complete state of defence. Breastworks were raised round the coast, batteries erected in every bay, Fort George efficiently strengthened, and the militia brought into a state of discipline and perfection. But the surviving good effected by this great man was the construction of new *military roads* the greatest boon ever conferred on the island ; which he not only planned and carried out, though strongly and ignorantly opposed at every step by the country people, who are so much benefited by it, but through his intercession with the Government, the 5,000*l.* gained by the sale of the Vale lands was appropriated to the construction of the roads commenced in 1810, extending to about eleven miles. Those constructed were from St. Peter Port to Vazon by the Rohais, Câtel, &c., and from the town to Le Rée by the Fort, St. Martin's, the Forest, &c.

The former state of these thoroughfares, Duncan thus describes:-

"Antecedently to the new roads first projected by Sir John Doyle in 1810, nothing had been done by art or science towards the least improvement of the island, nothing for the display of local beauties or advantages had been effected: there was not a road, or even an approach to the town where two carts could pass abreast ; the deep roads, only four feet six inches wide, with a footway of two or three feet, from which nothing but the steep banks on either side could be seen, appeared solely calculated for drains of water, which, running over them, rendered them every year deeper and narrower. There was not a vehicle, scarcely a horse, kept for hire ; no four-wheeled carriages existed ; and the traveller, landing in a town of lofty houses, confined and miserably-paved streets, from which he could only penetrate into the country by worse roads, left the island in haste and disgust, and under the most unfavourable impressions."

The column stands ninety-six feet in height, and about four hundred feet above the level of the sea: there is a spiral staircase ascending to the top, on which is a square gallery, secured by railings, whence the prospect is truly magnificent. The key of the entrance to the tower is kept at a neighbouring cottage, and can be had for a small gratuity.

Continuing his route two or three hundred yards, the visitor will pass the Jerbourg barracks, now unoccupied, and reach St. Martin's Point, on the promontory of

Jerbourg.

This has been thought by some historians to have been a Roman station, and thence to have derived its name from Cæsaris burgum, Jer, Ger, or Cher being a contraction of the word Cæsar ; and the fact of several Roman coins having been discovered here strengthened the supposition, which the more experienced chroniclers utterly repudiate: there are the remains of fortifications which no doubt belong to an ancient castle standing here in 1328, as appears by a mandate of King Edward III., of that date, directing its completion. As long ago as this early period the fief of Jerbourg belonged to an ancestor of the De Saumarez family ; and it was subsequently incorporated with that of Saumarez before mentioned the lord of the manor still bearing the title of hereditary châtelain of Jerbourg.

It is almost appalling to approach the precipitous line of cliffs at this spot ; but on recovering from the first shock the grandeur of the scenery impresses the mind with a sense of unrivalled magnificence. Continuing to the right along this mountain pass, the beautiful

Bay of Moulin Houet

will be seen below.

But the far more preferable approaches to this spot, the most picturesque in the whole island are *three* in number: one, by a narrow lane eastward of the estate of De Vic Carey, Esq., called the Vallon, the garden wall of which is to be skirted as far as the cliffs immediately above the bay ; another, about half a mile to the westward, is the main approach, which any cottager will point out. A gradual descent and a sudden turn of the lane brings the bay in sight. Below lies the sea, of a deeper blue than the heavens, except where the yellow sands turn its transparent waters green ; while, in bright contrast, the furze-brake on the opposite hill-side dazzles the eye in early spring, and again in autumn, with a blaze of gorgeous orange—the veritable "Field of the Cloth of Gold."

You pause in admiration of the magnificence and gentler graces of this spot ; then, descending lower, to a still lofty ledge of rock, the azure waters are seen changing into different hues as they approach the shallows and the white sweep of the sands ; the rugged reefs of granite appear around, above, and below ; and the purple masses of the opposite cliffs unfold a panorama more fitting for the artist's pencil than the feeble description of the pen. I have only alluded to one phase of this scene. Under every different aspect of sun, sky, and sea ; new and grander beauties will develop themselves ; and it is only by a personal visit, and that oft repeated, that the charms of this enchanting spot can be fully appreciated. About halfway down this approach, where a little tributary joins the streamlet that turns the mill at the bottom of the valley, is a "watery lane," which forms the third mode of access to this bay. This is to be found by taking the lane exactly opposite the windmill, on the road from St. Martin, at a place called "La Fontaine." Proceed then through a narrow lane, where a rivulet contends for the rustic pathway, and trees, laden with ivy, contrast their deep shade with the golden gleams of sunlight, which glitter amid a thousand shadows on innumerable ferns, luxuriating on the banks of the brook. The tourist is recommended either to come or return by this route.

The finest example of wild scenery is to be found in the vicinity of the bay: the peculiar forms assumed by the rocks and the detached masses in the sea are, in some instances, apparently the result of weathering, and in others of the mechanical action of the waves. It is inconceivable that some of the wild-looking forms which stand in grizzly majesty out of the waters were of their present shape when first produced ; the action of the elements, and the attacking force of the waves, have sculptured them, as with Nature's own hand, into their fantastic shapes. The summit of the tall cliffs on the eastern side is broken into singular turreted masses, between which intervals are left, so as to give to the rocks the almost exact resemblance to a ruined fortress, which is heightened by the luxuriant growth of mosses, lichens, and ivy climbing over the mimic masonry. This part is appropriately called the Castle, and there is one of equal similitude towering over the narrow footway as you pass through the little gate on the cliff facing the bay. Those four black, strange-looking rocks which project like a vast pier in ruins across the mouth of the bay—known as the "Needles," or the "Stacks of Peas,"—appear to have been at some previous time united, and to have formed a lofty and magnificent natural breakwater to this bay : they are of gneiss, and the action of the elements above, and of the waves below, appears to have washed away the softer portions—which united them. The summit of one of this beautiful group wears a grotesque resemblance to a human head when seen in certain directions ; while from another of them a curious detached piece of rock projects from near the top at an angle of almost precisely forty-five degrees. In consequence of the unequal durability of many of the rocks ; and of the abrading influence of the powerful waves which dash upon them, they are occasionally met with carved into the most singular shapes. At one point of this coast is a black mass of hornblende fashioned into the rude semblance of a gigantic beast couchant, and guarding the narrow entrance to a cave extending a little way into the cliffs, and nearly filled with water at high tide: when the waves rise foaming over this mass of rock a most picturesque appearance is given to it.

The cliffs forming the sides of this bay are in many places quite perpendicular and smooth as a wall, while in others they appear nodding to their fall. Ledges of uneven rocks project into the water at intervals of a few yards, leaving little creeks and narrow passages of great intricacy ; but it is quite unsafe to penetrate among them when the tide is rising, as then access to a safe part of the bay becomes intercepted by the water surrounding these sea-ward masses of rock, and escape is very difficult, and in some places might be impossible. At spring-tides, however, the sea retires to a considerable distance, and here, at low water, abound those beautiful rock-pools of which we have elsewhere spoken. These are on a larger scale, scattered about in every indentation of the generally submerged rocks, some half hidden amidst deep recesses, and opening to the sea through a vista of dark, rocky masses, still wet with the waters which for ages have been polishing down their once rugged surface. In such pellucid depths beautiful zoophytes display their flower-like arms with pink-brown, and blood-red hues, making beautiful the grey rocks on which they rest. The seaweeds there also wave their variously-coloured foliage, some green, some red, but mostly of an olive tint. Among them, lurking out of sight, minute fishes lie, now and then darting about, and again hiding under the leaves of the sea plants. Limpets abound on the rocks at their edges and in the fissures are to be found microscopic shells for a whole day's study and delight.

There is a small cottage on the cliffs, where, as well as at the mill beyond, visitors who bring their provisions can be accommodated with hot water, &c., and where many parties of pleasure are glad to rest themselves.

The pathway on the extreme point to the left leads, much under a mile, to the little harbourage of

Saint's Bay.

The road to this bay is a short distance west of that to Moulin Houet, turning to the left of that leading to *Icart Point*, and any peasant will direct you to it. It was naturally to be expected that in Guernsey, par excellence "La bien heureuse Isle Sainte," the name given to it by the monks when they came to the island in 996, we should find one of its bays of that nomenclature which prevails so generally throughout the island ; and seeking for a reason why this bay in particular had been so canonized, we were delighted in discovering among the rocks which abut on its eastern boundary the distinct form of three figures, having the semblance of two monks giving absolution, or, at any rate ablution, to a kneeling form beside them. Elated with our research, we sat down, as satisfied as an antiquary at the discovery of an ancient crypt ; but our enthusiasm was grievously disconcerted on ascertaining that "the true name of this bay and the country in its vicinity is *Sein*, not Saint."

There, nevertheless, our granite holy father stands, preaching "sermons in stones ;" and the visitor may mark their saint-like attitudes from the side of the martello tower, looking eastward across the bay.

Icart Point,

which lies half a mile to the westward, is a wild, sea-scathed district, devoid of all cultivation, and giving feed to a few scattered sheep with its scanty herbage. It will, however, well repay the pains of a visit, for the new and imposing view it presents of both the bays of Moulin Houet and of Petit Bôt, and of the Southern Cliffs, while its own crags and rocky precipices partake of the grand and beautiful, defying any approach to its shores. We have given a description of the last remaining bay on this the southern side in our subsequent excursion to *Petit Bôt Bay* ; and supposing our visitor to have had full enjoyment of these charming scenes in those we have lingered through to-day, we proceed homeward by the conspicuous object before us,

St. Martin's Church.

This sacred edifice presents the same sombre aspect which so much prevails among the parish churches of the island, and is devoid of all architectural attraction: a most uncouth figure forms one of the posts to the gateway entering to the churchyard, said to be "an idol of the aboriginal inhabitants."

The road to the town is now a short one of about a mile and a half by either route the visitor may take, either returning through the churchyard on foot, or by the road to the right or left ; the one will lead to Mount Row, and thence to the Grange and town, the other to the Fort, and by George Road to Hautville.

Above: Victor Hugo seated in an open carriage [calèche]
outside Sausmarez Manor (Guernsey Museum & Art Gallery)
Below: Fermain Bay

Above: St Martin's Avenue [Fort Road with Sausmarez Manor on the left]
Below: Doyle Column

147 GUERNSEY. — *Jerbourg.* — *Doyle Monument.* — *Jerbourg.* — *La Colonne Doyle.* — LL.

At Jerbourg, looking towards Moulin Huet.

Above: At Jerbourg looking towards Moulin Huet
Below: Moulin Huet

2835. 21. *Moulin Huet, Water Lane, Guernsey.*

Above: Maison du Guet, Moulin Huet (T. Singleton)
Below: Pierre Auguste Renoir, 'Brouillard à Guernesey'

Above: Hugo and party picnic at Maison du Guet

*('Groupe de personnages en promenade à Guernesey
avec la famille Hugo vers 1860',
Album de photographies prises à Jersey et à Guernesey, Folio 36 verso d.
© RMN-Grand Palais (musée d'Orsay) / Hervé Lewandowski)*

164 GUERNSEY. — Moulin Huet Bay. — Moulin Huet. - Les Rochers de la Plage. — LL.

Above: Moulin Huet Bay
Below: Cliff path at Moulin Huet

72.Path round the Cliffs, Moulin Huet, Guernsey.

Above: Saints Bay
Below: Saints Bay – Children on the sands

La Gran'mère du Chimquière, St Martin's Church
The stone is understood to have represented a goddess
and has been linked to a fertility cult.

EXCURSION 1: COMMENTARY

Early in his exile Hugo came to know this area well. He frequently walked to **Fermain** in the afternoon and swam there many times. In 1863 he had taken eight bathes by 6 August. The following year his first bathe was on 19 July. He enjoyed relaxing, sometimes composing poems. He found that he could write here –

... j'ai pour écrire une espèce de fauteuil naturel dans un rocher en un bel endroit appelé Firmain-bay. (Letter to Octave Lecroix, 30 June 1862). [*... for writing I have a kind of natural armchair in a rock in a beautiful place called Fermain Bay*].

In May one year while at the bay he wrote a letter to Juliette Drouet -

How to avoid dreaming about your approaching birthday? Here all nature is beautiful; the land is like a great green flower, the sea like a great blue flower, the sun-filled sky is like a great golden flower; a vast hope of happiness comes out of everything; to you I send it. The birds sing, the beach sings, the plain and the hill laugh, and there I am, alone, dreaming of you; and for me, in all this infinity, there is the thought of you, just as yesterday evening in that vast twilight sky that we gazed at together there was a very small star that shone by itself more than the whole sky... [M xiv/1326].

On 8 September 1860 he held a family picnic at the bay. Sometimes there were more intimate moments. On 2 December 1860 he walked along Fermain Bay. There was rain and mist. But, thanks to a sea breeze, he saw the very shapely legs of a very pretty girl. On 18 October 1861 he met up with a female first encountered at L'Hyvreuse in St Peter Port. He recorded the episode in his Agenda in Spanish, his language for sexual congress – *la del'Hyvreuse toda tomada*. [M xii/1342; M xii/1371; M xii/1510].

Mrs James de Havilland stumbled across Hugo on an occasion when he was accompanied by Juliette Drouet –

It was once my good fortune to see Victor Hugo in a moment of inspiration. He and Mme. Drouet walked together every afternoon, generally to Fermain Bay, then a most wild and lovely spot, whence on a fine day there is a good view of the French coast. One day I was alone on these cliffs, drinking in the marvellous beauty and colouring of rock and sea, when, from the other side of a ruined cottage, came a sort of chant. I went round softly, and there were Mme. Drouet and Victor Hugo, she with her head bent and her hands clasped as if in prayer, he with his hat off and a look I shall never forget of rhapsody and longing, in his grand face. The chant went on, evidently an appeal to the beloved "Patrie," rising and falling in a sort of rhythmic cadence. I stole quietly away for I felt that it was holy ground; but this glimpse of him in his inspired moments, made me understand the marvellous fascination he exercised over his generation. [de Havilland p.7].

In *L'Archipel* Hugo made mention of the **Doyle Column** –

Guernsey built a great column and dedicated it to its General; it overlooks the sea and can be seen from the Caskets. [M xii/533].

Hugo enjoyed sitting on a bench overlooking **Moulin Huet**. Sir Victor Carey told A. Bourde de la Rogerie –

I often saw Victor Hugo sitting on that bench. He would stay there for a long, long time, contemplating the ocean, gazing somewhere way out to sea, lost in the sea, in his dreams. [*Victor Hugo à Guernesey*, Avranches 1944, pp 5-6].

VH went on several picnic trips to this area. There was a grand picnic on 29 June 1859. Hugo recorded the attendance of Juliette Drouet, the Duverdiers, Miss Joss, Dr Terrier, Mme Ménage, the Marquands, Guérin, Miss Allix, Kesler, Dujardin, Lefèvre, small children, Charles, and himself. The party was a mixture of family, French refugees, and Guernsey friends. [M x/1483]. On 4 July 1859 Charles Hugo wrote to his mother –

> Eighteen of us have just been for a picnic at Moulin Huet. The fare was prepared by a French pastry-cook; cold leg of lamb, cold beef à la mode, ham, vol-au-vent, pigeon pie, and six bottles of iced champagne. The doctor and Marquand got tipsy, but the rest of the company remained within the bounds of cheerfulness. [*Victor Hugo en exil, catalogue of exhibition at Hauteville House*, 1955, p. 67.]

A photograph records the event and shows that the party made use of the cottage mentioned by Dally 'where visitors who bring their provisions can be accommodated with hot water, &c., and where many parties of pleasure are glad to rest themselves.' On 24 July 1870 Hugo and a group spent time on a Sunday at Moulin Huet. They bathed and dined *sous la baraque* – perhaps a reference to the cottage. They returned home at 10 p.m. Renoir admired the beauty of Moulin Huet and immortalised it in a series of paintings executed in September-October 1883. *Renoir in Guernsey* (States of Guernsey, 1988) provides an excellent discussion.

In *L'Archipel* Hugo ventured that **St Martin's** *passe pour une petite Nice* – high praise indeed. He noted the prehistoric monument at the gate of the parish church, dating it to the sixth century in *L'Archipel*; to the seventh century in his *Agenda* (M xii/531; M xiv/1435). On 6 November 1864, as evening drew on, Hugo encountered 'une folle' laughing at the entrance to the cemetery. Hugo lost sight of her as she disappeared among the tombs. [M xii/1472].

The mill at St Martin's was damaged in a storm in January 1863. Hugo often referred to it in his itineraries. On 16 May 1870 he recorded in his *Agenda* that it was no longer broken. [M xiv/1475].

2: North East Coast, the land of Gilliatt

EXCURSION 2

The East Esplanade—Salerie Battery—Ivy Castle—St. Sampson Church—St. Sampson Harbour—The Vale Castle—Bordeaux Harbour—The Cromlechs ; L'Autel de Déhus—Le Tombeau de Grand Sarazin—Le Champ de l'Autel—La Rocque qui Sonne—La Chaire du Prêtre—The Druids' Temple—La Rocque Balan—L'Ancresse Common—The Race Course—The Vale Church—Le Braye du Valle—Fish Pond—Return to the Town.

The usual road to St. Sampson is by the sea-side. Three omnibuses ply constantly between that harbour and St. Peter Port ; their stand is at the town church, and the fare is fivepence. The walk is, however, so beautiful that many would prefer it.

The route lies through Pollet Street, where an old house will be seen on the lea called "La Plaiderie," formerly the royal court-house. The *public baths* are on the right, in addition to which several bathing-machines are available at moderate charges.

The Pollet leads to the esplanade, a marine wall constructed in 1826 as a breakwater. At the east end is a battery called La Salerie, mounting four guns, on a little headland which gives shelter to fishing-boats. From the sea-wall there is a view of surpassing beauty, including the small islands of Herm and Jethou with Sark in the distance, and the sea-girt fortress of Castle Cornet, the town and its uplands. On low ground to the lea, about a mile from the town, stands

Ivy Castle.

There is little to interest the stranger in visiting this relic of antiquity. It was formerly called *Le Chateau des Marais*, from its situation in marshy land, and said to have been built in 1036 under the auspices of Robert Duke of Normandy, surnamed Le Diable, in grateful return for hospitalities afforded to him, when, a violent storm having scattered his fleet and driven him to anchor in a bay to the north of the island, the abbot and monks of St. Michael received and sheltered him. The castle, however, has not even survived its name, and the ivy has "claimed it for her own:" the walls alone are standing, but traces of the fosse are still visible, and remains of an outer wall and vallum, enclosing a space of about four acres, prove it to have been a stronghold of considerable consequence. Resuming your course by the sea-wall, another mile brings you to

St. Sampson Church.

St . Sampson, who was considered in earlier days as the patron saint of Guernsey, landed near this spot, where he caused a chapel to be erected, which was rebuilt in 1111, and raised to the rank of a parochial church and dedicated to his memory. It is the earliest church in the island, but subsequent alterations have left little of the original structure. The interior is quite plain, but bearing evidence of two distinct orders of architecture—the Early Norman, and the Early English : the nave and aisles are vaulted, as are all the churches in the island.

The church faces and abuts on

St. Sampson Harbour,

stated to be the only one used in early days, but now of secondary consequence, being principally used for the exportation of the excellent granite, which we have before stated to abound in this neighbourhood, in which article a considerable trade is carried on. The usual prices of stone delivered alongside of the vessel at St. Sampson are—

Spalls, or chippings of all sizes, broken for the purpose of macadamizing roads, 2*s*. 2*d*. per ton.

The same broken ready for laying, 4*s*. 6*d*. to 4*s*. 8*d*.

Paving or pitching stone,		3 in.	17*s*. per ton.
Ditto	ditto	4 in.	13*s*. per ton.
Ditto	ditto	5 in.	11*s*. per ton.
Ditto	ditto	6 in.	9*s*. per ton.
Common pitchers		...	8*s*. per ton.
Kerb-stone,	12 in. by 6 in.		8*d*. per foot lineal.
Ditto	12 in. by 8 in.		1*s*. per foot lineal.

Freights to London vary according to the demand, from 6*s*. 6*d*. to 7*s*. 6*d*. per ton.

The Vale Castle,

on the north, overlooks the harbour. It is said to have been built by order of a body of monks who emigrated from Normandy in the tenth century, as a place of refuge from the inroads of the pirates who infested the Channel. But little of the ancient castle now remains beyond its walls, gateway, and ramparts: the interior has been subsequently fitted up as a barrack ; in which, through infrequent use, the rooms have a most cheerless and uncomfortable aspect, only to be surpassed by the ugliness which their roofs and chimneys impart to the exterior of so noble a structure.

The lover of the picturesque should descend from the castle mound, by the narrow pathway, on the contrary side to the gateway, which will lead him by the prettily wooded seat of Mr. Advocate Falla, called "Les Roques Barices," in a walk of about a quarter of a mile to Bordeaux Harbour.

The visitor must, nothing daunted by its rough approach, not suffer one nook or corner of this sweet sequestered bay to remain unexplored : at high or low water there are a thousand allurements for whiling away a whole summer's day. Proceed to the full extent of the rugged footway across those patches of turf till you reach the farthest promontory to the east ; climb its mimic heights, and there—poet, painter, or dreamer—"sup your full," among those chasms of rocks scattered in wild confusion, and the surges that boil and bellow beneath. The tidal stream runs so strong and so high here, that many of the extreme masses of rock, on which you may sit with safety for an hour or two, are quite isolated, and some completely covered at high water ; inspect every peak and fissure of them carefully, for nowhere do those nature painters, the lichen parasites, more beautifully blend their varied tints of gold, orange, green, and grey, than in this secluded spot, where they touch nothing they do not adorn.

As you return, before leaving the bay, stroll in by the little footpath under the sea-stunted trees, and a scene of rural and calm repose will greet you, with its quiet contrast to that you have just quitted: the old farm-house with its quaint appendages, the moss-covered walls, the thickly-crowded trees, of fantastic forms and ivy-burdened trunks and branches, form at every point impromptu pictures, chequered with light and shade and every phase of the beautiful ; many of which an eminent native artist, Mr. Naftel, has transferred to his canvas, and rendered them the "cynosure of wondering eyes," on the walls of the Exhibition of the Society of Painters in Water Colours, of which he is a distinguished member.

Lodgings may be obtained at several houses in the immediate neighbourhood, which is the only sea-side spot away from the town that boasts of such an advantage, and they are eagerly sought for during the summer months in this pleasant retreat.

In this immediate vicinity, at a place called Paradis, the narrow lane to which it is necessary to inquire for, is the cromlech known by the name of

"L'Autel de Déhus," or "Tu Dus."

It stands on an artificial mound or tumulus, round the verge of which several stones remain of those forming the original circle. It comprises a deep trench, divided into several distinct compartments. The first, covered with an immense cap-stone, forms a chamber of about fifteen feet square. Divided from this by a transverse set or stones is a narrow passage between the props, which leads to a square chamber on the north, over which is a single flat stone about seven feet square. The eastern extremity is closed by a large stone abutting on the road which runs near it. The length of the trench is thirty-eight feet, and the number of cap-stones is eight. That at the west end is a fine, well-proportioned block, nearly seventeen feet long, and weighing from fifteen to twenty tons. Not far hence are the remains of another "kist," called

"Le Tombeau de Grand Sarazin."

If the superstition of our forefathers alone saved some of these relics from profanation, the ignorance of their successors has caused them to be held less sacred, for it is related, concerning this, that a former proprietor, having ordered his workmen to seek for building stones to erect a barn, they inadvertently, during his absence, broke up the cap-stones which covered the whole. The return of the owner happily prevented the total destruction of these ancient remains.

There is another cromlech, or kist, in a field near St. Sampson Harbour, called

"Le Champ de L'Autel,"

which is said to have been preserved, though the ground has been quarried around it, through the well-timed warning given by the vendor to the purchaser of the property, that if he ever removed or injured the altar he would never after be happy or prosperous.

About half a mile from the Vale Church (about a mile to the westward), tradition tells us there once stood a sacred and miracle-working stone, called

"La Rocque qui Sonne."

All trace of this, except its name, had been lost sight of until 1837, when, after diligent search and well-directed excavations, one remaining cap-stone was dug out and exposed to view ; the locality indicating that a much more extended space had been devoted to the same purpose.

The "sounding-stone" could, however, be nowhere discovered ; one demi-dolmen alone remaining to mark the spot. This stone, which is about thirteen feet long, is supported on a prop to the south, and rests on the ground at the north end, having another vertical stone near it, the corresponding parts of which have disappeared. At a distance of about sixty feet to the eastward, four large props were examined, which are supposed to have been a portion of the outer circle: these are now buried beneath the sod. From accounts in the neighbourhood, it would appear that there were formerly eight or nine cap-stones, including the enormous "Rocque qui Sonne ;" so that these were probably the finest and most extensive Celtic remains in the island. Many of them must have been standing till within these fifty years, if the following tale, which it is said "the peasants invariably relate to strangers," is to be relied on.

It runs, that about forty years ago, the owner of "Le Courtil de la Rocque qui Sonne"—the Field of the Sounding Stone—being about to build a house, determined to make use of the idle stone ; and in spite of all warning, and to the great terror of the neighbours, he unscrupulously broke it up, and used it for supports and lintels to his door and windows. No immediate judgment fell upon the sacrilegious offender ; but in less than twelve months his new house was burned to the ground. He rebuilt it, and a second time, in a most unaccountable manner, it shared the same fate. Resolving not to hazard a third attempt he sold the stones and shipped them off for England ; but still the same fatality attended them : the vessel foundered at sea, and all on board perished. It is to be regretted that some such catastrophe had not happened long before, if such were required "to persuade the Guernsey-man that it is a perilous and evil thing to touch a cromlech ;" for that "otherwise," as the authoress whom we quote writes, "they had all, long ere this, been in cottage-walls and church-gateways."

In the parish of St. Sampson, on the hill called "La Grosse Hougue," is another small demi-dolmen, standing on the brow, and visible from both sides of the mound ; and at a short distance hence may be seen a stone pulpit, called

"La Chaire du Prêtre."

It stands on its natural bed, but appears to have been artificially wrought into shape, for what purpose is unknown ; though it is supposed to have belonged in some way to the chapel of St. Clair, which once stood in this neighbourhood.

The principal and finest cromlech, called

The Druids' Temple,

is reached through the gate at the Vale Church, crossing L'Ancresse Common, and ascending the brow of the hill overlooking L'Ancresse Bay, or the Bay of Anchorage, so called from the landing there of Robert Duke of Normandy and his shipwrecked followers. These very superb remains were covered by the drifting sands, which are still suffered to accumulate around them, until their accidental discovery in 1811 ; but it was not until 1837 that they were fully explored and exposed to view, at the expense and through the antiquarian zeal of Mr. Lukis. This cromlech is 45 feet in length, by 13 feet in width, and nearly 8 feet in height within the area at the western end, whence it gradually contracts on each side and at the top towards the eastern end. This space is covered by five larger and two smaller blocks of granite, which are not in contact : the western block is computed to weigh about 30 tons, it being nearly 17 feet long, 10½ feet wide, and 4½ feet thick ; and it was probably placed by means of rollers. The second block is 16 feet long, the third smaller, and so they gradually diminish to the seventh. On the floor, when opened in 1837, were found two layers, consisting of human bones, urns of coarse red and black clay, stone and clay amulets and beads, bone pins, &c. : the layers, like those of cists, being separated by flat fragments of granite : the lower stratum was laid on a rude pavement on the natural soil. The remains were deposited in a singular manner. The unburnt bones occupied either end of the floor ; the middle third being allotted to those which had been submitted to the action of fire : not a vestige of charcoal was to be detected with them. The bones of individual skeletons were heaped together confusedly, and each heap surrounded by a small ring of pebbles ; the urns, which were of remarkably rude shape and material, being near or within the rings. Some heaps consisted, as it were, of parents' and children's ashes mingled together ; for within the same ring of pebbles were the bones of persons of all ages. An unusual quantity of bones of very young children was found. The lower stratum only contained the burnt bones, among which likewise a few tusks of the boar, perhaps worn as trophies of the chase, and consigned to the fire with the hunter's dead body. Four flat disks, from six to twelve inches in diameter, and one in thickness, formed of the same ware as the urns, were also found, and doubtless served as lids to some of the urns, which had broad, flat edges. As these lids are furnished with central handles, it may be inferred that the urns were replenished from time to time ; the cromlech being a hollow vault or catacomb.

In no instance was the urn used to contain the ashes of the dead, and it was doubtless filled with liquid, or food, at the time of sepulture. About one hundred and fifty urns were removed from this cromlech ; some were quite entire, and of those broken many have been restored. As time and ages elapsed, and possibly, all memory of the departed became lost, their remains were removed to make room for others ; those so removed were placed in the intervals between the props and were lost to sight ; but further space being again required, many cart-loads of limpet-shells, and a little yellow clay, were strewn upon the original deposit, and flat stones, as already said, were placed over all to form a new floor.

Nearly in the middle of the plain below is another relic, a simple cap-stone, covering a part of a sepulchre or kistvaen, which, when examined in 1837, contained human bones and ashes, pottery, celts, and an arrow-head of stone. On the eastern part of the plain is another kistvaen, surrounded by various blocks of stone, and about one hundred yards thence is a portion of a circle, defined by the remaining upright stones, and near it several stone graves.

To the right is a cairn, or hougue, called to this day

"La Rocque Balan,"

inducing the opinion that a rocking or balancing stone once stood here ; and it is recorded that there was, not long ago, a logan stone in the neighbourhood of L'Ancresse.

Indeed, there is no doubt, from all these evidences, and many more which remain to be explored, that a large portion of this region was, like Salisbury Plain, devoted to the worship, the funeral rites, and the place of sepulture of the Druids, or, rather, of those Celtic tribes who adopted their forms and ceremonies. Dr. Lukis, of Guernsey, in his "Memoir on the Cromlechs of the Channel Islands," read before the Society of Antiquaries in 1853, observes, that "it is a generally-received opinion that the Celtæ were the authors and architects of these megaliths." Their very extensive existence in Guernsey proves, therefore, that the island was inhabited long before the Christian era, having been first peopled from Gaul, when it was yet plunged in the grossest superstition and barbarism. Mr. Tupper remarks, that "the origin of Druid worship may be first traced to the east, afterwards diversified to suit the more northern notions of the Celts. The Druids did not admit of idols, and they believed in the immortality of the soul. The earliest notice of the Celts places them about the year 500 B.C., in the neighbourhood of the Pyrenees, whence they were driven into that part of Gaul where they were found in the time of Cæsar. The Celts were a people of an inferior stature, swarthy in complexion, with dark eyes, and hair short, coarse, and black. This description applies to many of the peasantry in "the most remote, or southern parishes of Guernsey, in whom the Celtic blood is very manifest."

L'Ancresse Common

lies before you on leaving the last-named cromlech. THE RACES are held here in July, on which occasion Her Majesty gives a cup to be run for by island-bred horses.

The Vale Church

stands at the entrance to L'Ancresse. It was erected in 1117, close to the ancient Priory of St. Michael, part of the south wall of the churchyard and of the adjoining farm-house being all that remains of the ancient building, though the latter still bears the name of *L'Abbaye*. There is a huge mass of stone to the west of the church, apparently the cap-stone to a cromlech. The church consists of two chancels and aisles, western tower, vestry, a chapel on the north side, and northern porch.

The visitor may hence retrace his steps, or his vehicle, by a good road of three miles to the town ; but fifty-five years ago he would have found himself in the unpleasant predicament of being stopped in his career at this spot by an *arm* of the sea. In the old charts, Guernsey is delineated as two islands, being divided, at high water, by a narrow channel, of which the eastern end was at St. Sampson Harbour, and the western at Grande Havre, near the Vale Church.

In 1803 a tract of land, comprising about 300 acres, known as "LE BRAYE DU VALLE," was overflowed by the sea at high water ; and the then lieutenant-governor, Sir John Doyle, seeing the danger the island would incur should the enemy attempt or effect a landing in L'Ancresse Bay, when the passage, by reason of a high tide, would be impracticable for troops, recommended to Government the exclusion of the sea by the erection of strong embankments at both ends. The result was the recovery of a valuable tract, which realized 5,000*l.* ; and corn and crops now grow, and farm-houses are erected, where, at the commencement of this century, rolled the waves of the Atlantic.

The large pond near the church is principally supplied from the drainage of the adjacent fields, but it is occasionally subject to incursions from the sea, which finds its way at spring-tides through the flood-gates. Excellent fishing maybe had here by permission of the owner ; and on the occasion of the pond being periodically drained, an abundance of fish is taken. The water is generally so little brackish, that cattle drink it freely ; and yet several of the salt-water fish, the grey mullet in particular, are said to thrive and fatten in it to perfection. Turbots, plaice, soles, bass, whitings, cod, and smelts, are all to be found here, and more especially the fresh-water eel, which is rare in the island, is caught in abundance.

St Peter Port from Hougue à la Perre, Guernsey

Above: Tower No 1 at Hougue à la Perre
Below: The solitary survivor of the Basses Maisons,
Grand Bouet (Photo: Michael Paul)

Above: St Sampson's harbour
Below: A Quarry at St Sampson's

VIEW OF A QUARRY AT ST SAMPSON'S, GUERNSEY.

Above: St Sampson's Church (Henry Wimbush)
Below: St Sampson's (Moss Print)

Above: Vale Castle (Berry)
Below: View of Houmet Paradis from Vale Castle (Photo: Michael Paul)

Above: Bordeaux Harbour (Henry Wimbush)
Below: La Rocque qui Sonne (photo: Andrew Fothergill)

Above: Victorian tourists visit the Druids' Altar, L'Ancresse Common.
Below: Thomas Singleton's photo of the same site, now known as
La Varde dolmen

Hugo's fiction and its factual inspiration:

Left: 'Gild-Holm-'Ur Seat',
Les Travailleurs de la Mer

Below: Chaire du Prêtre
(Lukis Collection,
Guernsey Museum
& Art Gallery)

Above: Le Tombeau du Grand Sarrazin
(Lukis Collection, Guernsey Museum & Art Gallery)
Below: Ivy Castle (Berry)

EXCURSION 2: COMMENTARY

Hugo frequently travelled this route. Usually he went in an 'anti-clockwise' direction from St Peter Port to St Sampson and then north to L'Ancresse (as Dally) but sometimes he travelled 'clockwise' – Coutanchez – la Braye du Valle – L'Ancresse – St Sampson – St Peter Port. In his carriage excursions Hugo regularly covered all the territory described by Dally. As we shall see, at least once he walked to the prehistoric monuments at L'Ancresse.

Dally's itinerary began at **Salerie Corner**. In Hugo's day there were decaying buildings there and they inspired his description of old St Malo. For a full treatment see Cox *Victor Hugo's St Peter Port* Blue Ormer, 2018, pp.83-85.

When jotting down this itinerary Hugo sometimes called it *le pays de Gilliatt*. That is an excellent title. The opening chapter and the last chapter of *The Toilers of the Sea* are located here. We shall follow Gilliatt's movements, with occasional interpellations from *L'Archipel* and elsewhere.

The novel begins on the road leading north from St Peter Port. The road was almost deserted. Throughout that portion of the highway which separates the first from the second tower, only three pedestrians could be seen.

The towers were defence fortifications. In the late 18th century the British built loophole towers to protect beaches from invasion. The towers were constructed 30 feet high and 20 feet in diameter. The fifteen towers are numbered in a sequence starting from St Peter Port and progressing in a counter-clockwise direction.

Hugo here refers to towers 1 and 2. They no longer exist. However, there are towers that have survived. In the description of Gilliatt's voyage around the coast of Guernsey Hugo mentions towers 6 and 7 (see p. 84 below). These are situated on L'Ancresse Common in the

Vale. Hugo would also have been familiar with towers 13 (Petit Bôt), 14 (Saints Bay), and 15 (St Martin).

> Suddenly, near a group of oaks at the corner of a field, and at the spot called the **Basses Maisons**, Déruchette turned, and the movement seemed to attract the attention of the man [Gilliatt]. She stopped, seemed to reflect a moment, then stooped, and the man fancied that he could discern that she was tracing with her finger some letters in the snow. Then she rose again, went on her way at a quicker pace, turned once more, this time smiling, and disappeared to the left of the roadway, by the footpath under the hedges which leads to the **Ivy Castle**. When she had turned for the second time, the man had recognised her as Déruchette, a charming girl of that neighbourhood. [*Toilers* I/i/1].

With neat symmetry Hugo revisits the scene at the end of the novel.

> Suddenly he stopped, and, turning his back, contemplated for some minutes a group of oaks beyond the rocks which concealed the road to Vale. They were the oaks at the spot called the **Basses Maisons**. It was there that Déruchette once wrote with her finger the name of Gilliatt in the snow. Many a day had passed since that snow had melted away. [*Toilers* III/iii/5].

Gilliatt's final journey to St Sampson is an opportunity for Hugo to celebrate Guernsey's natural history –

> The day was beautiful; more beautiful than any that had yet been seen that year. It was one of those spring days when May suddenly pours forth all its beauty, and when nature seems to have no thought but to rejoice and be happy. Amidst the many murmurs from forest and village, from the sea and the air, a sound of cooing could be distinguished. The first butterflies of the year were resting on the early roses. Everything in

nature seemed new—the grass, the mosses, the leaves, the perfumes, the rays of light. The sun shone as if it had never shone before. The pebbles seemed bathed in coolness. Birds but lately fledged sang out their deep notes from the trees, or fluttered among the boughs in their attempts to use their new-found wings. There was a chattering all together of goldfinches, pewits, tomtits, woodpeckers, bullfinches, and thrushes. The blossoms of lilacs, May lilies, daphnes, and melilots mingled their various hues in the thickets. A beautiful kind of water-weed peculiar to Guernsey covered the pools with an emerald green; where the kingfishers and the water-wagtails, which make such graceful little nests, came down to bathe their wings. Through every opening in the branches appeared the deep blue sky. A few lazy clouds followed each other in the azure depths. The ear seemed to catch the sound of kisses sent from invisible lips. Every old wall had its tufts of wallflowers. The plum-trees and laburnums were in blossom; their white and yellow masses gleamed through the interlacing boughs. The spring showered all her gold and silver on the woods. The new shoots and leaves were green and fresh. Calls of welcome were in the air; the approaching summer opened her hospitable doors for birds coming from afar. It was the time of the arrival of the swallows. The clusters of furze-bushes bordered the steep sides of hollow roads in anticipation of the clusters of the hawthorn. The pretty and the beautiful reigned side by side; the magnificent and the graceful, the great and the little, had each their place. No note in the great concert of nature was lost. Green microscopic beauties took their place in the vast universal plan in which all seemed distinguishable as in limpid water. Everywhere a divine fulness, a mysterious sense of expansion, suggested the unseen effort of the sap in movement. Guttering things glittered more than ever; loving natures became more tender. There was a hymn in the flowers, and a radiance in the sounds of the air. The wide-diffused harmony of nature burst forth on every side. All things which felt the dawn of life invited others to put forth shoots. A movement coming from below, and also from above, stirred vaguely all hearts susceptible to the scattered and subterranean influence of germination. The flower shadowed forth the fruit; young maidens dreamed of love. It was nature's universal bridal. It was fine, bright, and warm; through the hedges in the meadows children were seen laughing and playing at their games. The fruit-trees filled the orchards with their heaps of white and pink blossom. In the fields were primroses, cowslips, milfoil, daffodils, daisies, speedwell, jacinths, and violets. Blue borage and yellow irises swarmed with those beautiful little pink stars which flower always in groups, and are hence called 'companions.' Creatures with golden scales glided between the stones. The flowering houseleek covered the thatched roofs with purple patches. Women were plaiting hives in the open air; and the bees were abroad, mingling their humming with the murmurs from the sea. Nature, sensitive to the touch of spring, exhaled delight. [*Toilers* III/iii/5].

Guernsey blossoming with new life, a scene that Hugo describes with the precision of a scientist and the sensibility of a poet. The scene has an added poignancy. The beauty of the scene is in counterpoint to the tragic context. Gilliatt is walking to the coast where he will see his beloved Déruchette sailing away, where his life will end.

When Gilliatt arrived at St. Sampson, the water had not yet risen at the further end of the harbour, and he was able to cross it dry-footed unperceived behind the hulls of vessels fixed for repair. A number of flat stones were placed there at regular distances to make a causeway. [*Toilers* III/iii/5].

Hugo had presented his readers with a brief history of St Sampson earlier in the novel –

The **St Sampson** of the present day is almost a city; the St

Sampson of forty years since was almost a village...The people of St Sampson, except a few rich families among the townsfolk, are also a population of quarriers and carpenters. The port is a port of ship repairing. The quarrying of stone and the fashioning of timber go on all day long; here the labourer with the pickaxe, there the workman with the mallet. At night they sink with fatigue, and sleep like lead. Rude labours bring heavy slumbers.

... Nine had already struck in the old Romanesque belfry, surrounded by ivy, which shares with the church of St. Brélade at Jersey the peculiarity of having for its date four ones (IIII), which are used to signify eleven hundred and eleven. [*Toilers* III/i/1].

Having passed through St Sampson, Gilliatt carried on northwards:

He soon went on his way, climbed the hill of Vale Castle, descended again...

Hugo knew **Vale Castle**. On 25 June 1863 [M xii/1426] he went there with Jules Bastide (sometime a minister in the French government). In retracing Gilliatt's journey we must remember that in the 1820s, and also in Hugo's day, there was no coastal road to the east of the castle. Hence Gilliatt's journey over the hill. He

directed his steps towards the Bû de la Rue. The Houmet-Paradis was a solitude. [*Toilers* III/iii/5].

Bû de la Rue was Gilliatt's home –

It was situated at the extremity of a little promontory, rather of rock than of land, forming a small harbourage apart in the creek of Houmet Paradis. The water at this spot is deep. The house stood quite alone upon the point, almost separated from the island, and with just sufficient ground about it for a small garden, which was sometimes inundated by the high tides. Between the port of St. Sampson and the creek of Houmet Paradis, rises a steep hill, surmounted by the block of towers covered with ivy, and known as Vale Castle, or the Château de l'Archange; so that, at St. Sampson, the Bû de la Rue was shut out from sight. [*Toilers* I/i/2].

The Bû de la Rue no longer exists. Even the little peninsula on which his house stood has vanished, levelled by the pickaxe of the quarryman, and carried away, cart-load by cart-load, by dealers in rock and granite. It must be sought now in the churches, the palaces, and the quays of a great city. All that ridge of rocks has been long ago conveyed to London. [*Toilers* I/i/8].

In *L'Archipel de la Manche* Hugo imagined that the island might disappear through the sale of granite [M xii/538]. He was not indulging in hyperbolic fantasy, he was echoing his friend Henri Tupper –

… A limit to the export of stone must be reached at one time or another, otherwise we must suppose an amount of trade carried on which in a few years, if continual increase went on, would carry Guernsey away altogether. (*The Star*, 11 February 1864; report of Tupper's address to the Chamber of Commerce.)

Dally describes seven prehistoric sites. Hugo almost certainly was acquainted with them all and, as we shall see below, they inspired passages in *The Toilers of the Sea*. The granite export industry wrought havoc with these monuments and today the *Chaire du Prêtre* and the *Tombeau du Grand Sarrazin* are known to us solely through drawings executed by Lukis (see pp.60-61). Happily the Déhus and la Varde (the Druids' Temple) still survive. La Varde was probably the site visited by Hugo on his nocturnal expedition to the Vale with his brother-in-law (see below).

To return to the journey of Gilliatt. He eventually arrived at the **Gild-Holm-'Ur** seat, a natural seat 'hollowed out by the water and polished by the rains.'

> At the extremity of the ridge on which the Bû de la Rue was situated, was a large rock, which the fishing people of Houmet called the 'Beast's Horn.' This rock, a sort of pyramid, resembled, though less in height, the 'Pinnacle' of Jersey. At high water the sea divided it from the ridge, and the Horn stood alone; at low water it was approached by an isthmus of rocks. The remarkable feature of this 'Beast's Horn' was a sort of natural seat on the side next the sea, hollowed out by the water, and polished by the rains. The seat, however, was a treacherous one. The stranger was insensibly attracted to it by 'the beauty of the prospect,' as the Guernsey folks said. Something detained him there in spite of himself, for there is a charm in a wide view. The seat seemed to offer itself for his convenience; it formed a sort of niche in the peaked façade of the rock. To climb up to it was easy, for the sea, which had fashioned it out of its rocky base, had also cast beneath it, at convenient distances, a kind of natural stairs composed of flat stones.

Hugo may have been inspired by a monument at St Clair, *la Chaire du Prêtre*. It was some eight to ten feet in height and at the base was a large flat stone, giving the whole mass the appearance of a gigantic chair or pulpit (see page 60).

> Very old inhabitants of Guernsey used to call this niche fashioned in the rock by the waves, 'Gild-Holm-'Ur' seat, or Kidormur; a Celtic word, say some authorities, which those who understand Celtic cannot interpret, and which all who understand French can—'Qui-dort-meurt'; such is the country folks' translation. The reader may choose between the translation, Qui-dortmeurt, and that given in 1819, I believe in *The Armorican*, by M. Athenas. According to this

learned Celtic scholar, Gild- Holm-'Ur signifies 'The resting-place of birds.' [*Toilers* I/i/8].

Hugo is here indulging in a gentle parody. During the 1850s and 1860s the Guernsey newspapers not uncommonly carried letters from antiquaries discussing the origins of local place-names. There was room for debate – were the roots Celtic, Scandinavian, or French? Hugo creates his own fictional name and bedecks it with fictional philological speculation.

> Gilliatt haunted the druidical stones of **L'Ancresse**. He never went to chapel. He often went out at night-time. He held converse with sorcerers. He had been seen, on one occasion, sitting on the grass with an expression of astonishment on his features. He haunted the druidical stones of the Ancresse, and the fairy caverns which are scattered about in that part. It was generally believed that he had been seen politely saluting the *Roque qui Chante*, or Crowing Rock. [*Toilers* I/i/4].

Gilliatt sounds a trifle like Hugo, for he never attended church or chapel. Moreover Hugo went on a nocturnal expedition to the prehistoric monuments at L'Ancresse. It was recorded by Paul Chenay, his brother-in-law, who accompanied him. Filled with awe they approached five vast tombs. Hugo, greatly moved, began to stammer slowly, and in a low voice; then, as if inspired, his voice grew stronger, in harmony with the noise of the rising sea which accompanied his words. Chenay was the sole member of the audience at this unique symphony and recorded it enthusiastically. [Chenay, p.60].

Just as Gild-Holm-'Ur may have been inspired by *la Chaire du Prêtre*, so Hugo's *Roque qui Chante* is a fictional echo of *la Roque qui Sonne*. The story recounted by Dally is substantially accurate. Today only a few stones of *la Roque qui Sonne* survive (at Vale Primary School).

L'Ancresse receives a brief mention in *L'Archipel de la Manche* (xiii):

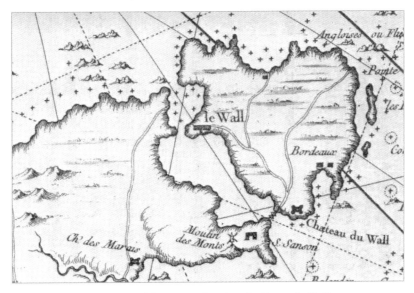

1757 Map of Guernsey showing the Braye du Valle

The huge L'Ancresse common is enclosed with gates that half naked children will open for a penny.

The return to St Peter Port took the traveller across the **Braye du Valle**, an area reclaimed from the sea during the Napoleonic era. Hugo explains –

> Until around 1805, Guernsey was divided into two islands. A salt river crossed it from one side to the other, from East Mount Crevel to West Mount Crevel. This sound came out in the west, opposite the Fruquiers and the two Sauts Roquiers; there were bays which penetrated far inland, one as far as Saltpans; they called this the Braye du Valle. In the last century, St Sampson's was an anchorage for boats on both sides of an ocean lane. It was a narrow and winding street. [M xii/539].

On 5 June 1869 Hugo returned to town via *environs du château de lierre* (Ivy Castle). [M xiv/1424]. Hugo took an interest in the medieval castles of Guernsey. He had a passion for the medieval era, its art and architecture. Alex J. Novikoff comments:

> ... although Hugo had no formal training in medieval history or literature, he truly ought to be considered something of a medievalist *avant la lettre*. He served on committees dedicated to the preservation of France's old buildings and wrote public opinion articles lambasting the architectural "vandals" who were tearing down medieval structures across the country in the name of progress and profit. [https://h-france.net/fffh/classics/medievalism-and-modernity-in-victor-hugos-hunchback-of-notre-dame/ Retrieved 10 March 2019.]

When the destruction of Vale Castle was threatened, Hugo gave support to his friend Henri Marquand (editor of *la Gazette de Guernesey*) who vigorously campaigned for the preservation of the castle. In February 1857 Marquand quoted Hugo in an editorial –

> L'autre jour, le restaurateur de l'Archéologie en Europe – Victor Hugo – nous disait que la destruction du château de l'Archange serait une profanation; une absurdité sans nom, et qu'aujourd'hui en Epire ou en Asie mineure, un pacha reculerait devant un pareil acte de vandalism.' [*Gazette*, February 1857].

> [*The other day the restorer of archaeology in Europe – Victor Hugo – said to us that the destruction of the Archangel castle* (i.e. Vale Castle) *would be a profanation; an absurdity without a name, and that today in Epirus or Asia Minor a pasha would recoil in the face of similar vandalism.*]

Islanders and visitors alike should remember Hugo as a strident defender of Guernsey's architectural heritage.

3: West Coast and 'Mon Île'

EXCURSION 3

Cobo Bay—Grand Rock—Monday's Hotel—Vazon Bay—Le Creux des Fées—The Gorban—La Descente des Aragonsais— King's Mills—Le Moulin du Milieu—Le Moulin du Haut—The Talbot Road—Return to the Town.

Cobo Bay.

The main road to this pretty and quiet retreat, with its beautiful sands, and rocky shores open to the Atlantic, is past the College, by the Grange, and thence for a mile by *Ivy Gate*, along the *Rohais Road*, keeping the main road on your right for another mile and a half till you pass through an avenue of trees, at the entrance to which four roads meet. On the right stands *Saumarez*, the seat of the Hon. Colonel Saumarez, and on the left an ancient estate, called the *Haye du Puits*, belonging to the Le Marchant family. The house has a grotesque French appearance, with its quaint turrets and vanes; the grounds behind are richly studded with ilex, of large growth : and on either side are timber trees, of luxuriant size, considering their proximity to the sea, to which and to the bay a short walk through this lane will conduct. The whole distance from the town is three miles.

A ramble on the sands to the rocky promontory, about a mile to the right, will well repay the exertion. It is called GRAND ROCK ; and on a sunny day you may rest here for hours in the enjoyment of its cool breezes and the music of its waters, lashing the granite barriers beneath: Here, as well as throughout the shore of the whole bay, the pools left at low water among the rocks form ready-made aquariums, in which the naturalist will find rare specimens of zoophitea, sponges, algæ, and other marine plants. The rocks themselves, too, deserve a close inspection, clothed as they are with lichen of every hue, and remarkable here for their peculiar stratification, which has produced steps as regular as if formed by the hand of man from their topmost height to the edge of the pools. The "samphire-gatherer" reaps his richest harvest among the fissures of these rocks, while the ground is studded with the "flowering thrift :" and in April and May the rare little bulb, *tricomena bulbicodium*, blossoms in great abundance.

Returning by Cobo Bay, the most extensive fishery in the island, at its south end, keeping to the shore, is a comfortable house for rest and refreshment,

Munday's Hotel;

and proceeding from thence, at a distance of a quarter of a mile, is

Vazon Bay

This beautiful bay extends from the point of land called *Le Hommet* at the north for about a mile, to that on which stand Richmond Barracks to the westward. On the first-named point a strong fortification is now being constructed by the Government ; and near this is

Le Creux des Fées,

or Fairies' Cave. It extends to a depth of about thirty or forty feet only. Of course, as its name imports, a number of wild fables have been associated with it, such as that it was formed by a band of fairies, and that it had a subterraneous communication with St. Saviour's Church, which stands on a hill more than two miles off;

in fact, the cave is of very limited extent.

The Corban, or Gorban.

This vegetable substance has been known to exist beneath the sands of Vazon Bay for a considerable period ; but it is nowhere visible on the surface. It is derived from a submerged forest, swallowed up by the encroachments of the sea ; and on its being discovered that this ligneous deposit was an excellent fuel, it received the singular scriptural title of corban, or gorban, as corrupted here, signifying "a gift"...

Vazon Bay is also interesting as the landing-place, in 1372, of a large body of French troops and levies from Spain, known in the chronicles as "*la descente des Aragossais.*"

The tourist should leave the bay at the *martello tower* and turn towards the *left*, which will bring him in less than half a mile to another spot where four roads meet : two of these take you back to the town, the first by the beautiful estate of St. George, the other through the village of the Câtel ; but unless that walk will suffice you for one day, proceed by the road to the right, and descend the hill half a mile on, to

King's Mills

This, by far the prettiest hamlet in the island, reminds one strongly of an English village : the view of it, from many points, with its range of hills on one side, capped with their three windmills, its level water-meadows stretching to the sea on the other, and its cottages peeping through the trees, is exceedingly rural and picturesque.

The peasantry seem to bestow more care here on their gardens than in most of the other parts of the island, where they are left without attentive cultivation by the cottagers, nature doing everything and man or woman little or nothing, except where they are grown and rudely and carelessly rooted up for market. *Here* there seems to exist a proper pride in their flowers ; myrtles and roses, with geraniums and jessamine, covering many a cottage wall and the gayer gifts of Flora brightening their well-trimmed borders. This superiority may be attributable to the sheltered situation of the village—for an orange-tree on each side of the door of a house at the end of the little street, bearing fruit in the open air, with but little shelter in the winter, attests the mild temperature of the locality.

You need not proceed beyond the village, as there is nothing of interest within a mile or two, and what there is, we reserve for another trip.

As you arrive, on returning through King's Mills, at the large, modern-built water-mills, near which are some old ivied walls, said to be the remains of a monastery, turn by the road to the right, and you will come to one of the more ancient mills called

Moulin du Milieu.,

and through a thickly-shaded lane, with the little stream that feeds the mills babbling at your side, and from which ferns of gigantic size and unrivalled beauty rear their stately and graceful forms, you arrive at the third mill,

Le Moulin du Haut.

The village takes its name from these three water-mills, the proprietors of which in feudal times claimed the sole right of grinding corn for their vassals, and held this privilege by doing suit and service to the Court of St. Michael, by presenting a plate of wheaten flour when it passed in procession.

Midway between these mills, you may enter, on the right, a narrow by-path, through the only wooded walk that the island boasts of ; and beautiful it is, as you ascend its winding pathway, which leads hither and thither to the shady covert, and now down again to the side of the tiny brook : here the lady-fern expands her bosom and extends her gracile arms to the royal-fern, who waves his flowery sceptre above her head, while thousands of their subjects bend beneath them in obeisance as they dip their garlands in the rivulet below, These woodland pathways lead you to the upper mill, passing which you may, if inclined, follow the track and ascend the hill—no very easy task—but, near the windmill on its summit, an extensive view of varied beauty—richly cultured land and boundless sea, shaded valley and wooded heights—well repays your toil and trouble.

There will be sufficient daylight left to return to town, still distant only about three miles by the road from the last-named water-mill. Passing the arched gateway of an old estate called *Grehoignet*, and leaving the first road to the right (which leads to St. Helene and St. Andrew's Church), you will enter the

Talbot Road,

which winds through an undulating valley of quiet beauty, its little stream supplying the overshot-wheels of two or three ancient mills. On emerging thence, pass the *next* road, and then, turning to the left, you arrive at the main thoroughfare to St. Andrew's, and passing the *Bailiff's Cross* by Mount Row, you arrive at the Queen's Road, which leads to the Grange, or you may continue your route by Mont Durand into the town.

We have been rather minute in these details, because such is by far the most interesting tour for the pedestrian ; but there are other modes of reaching King's Mills and its adjacent parts, which we proceed to describe.

On the Road to Cobo Bay, Guernsey

Above: On the Road to Cobo Bay
Below: Road near Cobo (T. Singleton)

Above: Washing near Vazon (Henry Wimbush)
Below: La Haye du Puits (Henry Wimbush)

Above: Le Guet (Paul Jacob Naftel, courtesy Martel Maides Auctions)
Below: Guernsey fisherman

Above: 'Mon Île' – Le Noir Houmet, Portinfer (Wendy Griffin)
Below: Lion Rock, Cobo (Henry Wimbush)

Above: Talbot Valley (Paul Jacob Naftel, Guernsey Museum & Art Gallery)
Below: Moulin des Niaux, Talbot Valley (photo: Chris George)

Excursion 3: Commentary

This was a favourite excursion of Hugo. It took him from the east of the island to the west. He noticed many differences and recorded them in *L'Archipel* –

> Guernsey, gracious on one side, is dreadful on the other. The West is ravaged, exposed to the blasts from the open sea. There, there are breakers, squalls, creeks where vessels can be beached, patched-up boats; fallow-land, moorland, tumbledown houses, an occasional low-lying, shivering hamlet, skinny livestock, short and salty grass, and an overall picture of great poverty. [M xii/517].

The architecture differed –

> You can see the two kinds of old French farm on Guernsey. On the east side, it's the Norman farm; on the west, the Breton farm; the Norman farm more architectural, the Breton farm with more trees. The Norman farm stores its harvests in barns; the Breton farm, more primitive, shelters its harvests under a thatched roof held up by rugged, almost cyclopean, pillars, misshapen stone cylinders filled in with Portland cement. [M xii/542].

The gardens differed –

> In the cottage gardens of the west, where the tempest has a free hand, the trees are on the defensive; they stoop and look knocked about, like athletes. No flowers in these gardens of the west; their ingenious owners make up for this with plaster statues. [M xii/543].

But not all was bleak –

> Small ponds, peculiar to low-lying ground, brighten up the

farms in the West. Close by are bays where vessels can be beached, with fishing boats scattered over the grass, *Julia, Piety, Seagull,* etc, propped up on four logs. Seagulls and ducks perch like brothers on the sides of these boats – the ducks coming from the ponds, the seagulls from the ocean. [M xii/543].

In *The Toilers of the Sea* Hugo uses the departure of Gilliatt (from the Vale for the Roches Douvres) to present a vivid portrait of activities on the north and west coasts –

On that same night, at different hours, and at different points, various persons scattered and isolated on the western coast of Guernsey, observed certain facts.

As the Omptolle fisherman was mooring his bark, a carter of seaweed about half-a-mile off, whipping his horses along the lonely road from the Clôtures near the Druid stones, and in the neighbourhood of the Martello Towers 6 and 7, saw far off at sea, in a part little frequented, because it requires much knowledge of the waters, and in the direction of North Rock and the Jablonneuse, a sail being hoisted. He paid little attention to the circumstance, not being a seaman, but a carter of seaweed.

Half-an-hour had perhaps elapsed since the carter had perceived this vessel, when a plasterer returning from his work in the town, and passing round Pelée Pool, found himself suddenly opposite a vessel sailing boldly among the rocks of the Quenon, the Rousse de Mer, and the Gripe de Rousse. The night was dark, but the sky was light over the sea, an effect common enough; and he could distinguish a great distance in every direction. There was no sail visible except this vessel.

A little lower, a gatherer of crayfish, preparing his fish wells on the beach which separates Port Soif from the Port Enfer, was puzzled to make out the movements of a vessel between the Boue Corneille and the Moubrette. The man must have been a good pilot, and in great haste to reach some destination to risk his boat there.

Just as eight o'clock was striking at the Catel, the tavern-keeper at Cobo Bay observed with astonishment a sail out beyond the Boue du Jardin and the Grunettes, and very near the Susanne and the Western Grunes.

Not far from Cobo Bay, upon the solitary point of the Houmet of Vason Bay, two lovers were lingering, hesitating before they parted for the night. The young woman addressed the young man with the words, "I am not going because I don't care to stay with you: I've a great deal to do." Their farewell kiss was interrupted by a good sized sailing boat which passed very near them, making for the direction of the Messellettes.

Monsieur le Peyre des Norgiots, an inhabitant of Cotillon Pipet, was engaged about nine o'clock in the evening in examining a hole made by some trespassers in the hedge of his property called La Jennerotte, and his "friquet planted with trees." Even while ascertaining the amount of the damage, he could not help observing a fishing-boat audaciously making its way round the Crocq Point at that hour of night.

On the morrow of a tempest, when there is always some agitation upon the sea, that route was extremely unsafe. It was rash to choose it, at least, unless the steersman knew all the channels by heart.

At half-past nine o'clock, at L'Equerrier, a trawler carrying home his net stopped for a time to observe between Colombelle and the Souffleresse something which looked like a boat. The boat was in a dangerous position. Sudden gusts of wind of a very dangerous kind are very common in that spot. The Souffleresse, or Blower, derives its name from the sudden gusts of wind which it seems to direct upon the vessels, which by rare chance find their way thither.

At the moment when the moon was rising, the tide being high and the sea being quiet, in the little strait of Li-Hou, the solitary keeper of the island of Li-Hou was considerably startled. A long black object slowly passed between the moon and him. This dark form, high and narrow, resembled a winding-sheet spread out and moving. It glided along the line of the top of the wall formed by the ridges of rock. The keeper of Li-Hou fancied that he had beheld the Black Lady.

The White Lady inhabits the Tau de Pez d'Amont; the Grey Lady, the Tau de Pez d'Aval; the Red Lady, the Silleuse, to the north of the Marquis Bank; and the Black Lady, the Grand Etacré, to the west of Li-Houmet. At night, when the moon shines, these ladies stalk abroad, and sometimes meet.

That dark form might undoubtedly be a sail. The long groups of rocks on which she appeared to be walking, might in fact be concealing the hull of a bark navigating behind them, and allowing only her sail to be seen. But the keeper asked himself, what bark would dare, at that hour, to venture herself between Li-Hou and the Pécheresses, and the Anguillières and Lérée Point? And what object could she have? It seemed to him much more probable that it was the Black Lady.

As the moon was passing the clock-tower of St. Peter in the Wood, the serjeant at Castle Rocquaine, while in the act of raising the drawbridge of the castle, distinguished at the end of the bay beyond the Haute Canée, but nearer than the Sambule, a sailing-vessel which seemed to be steadily dropping down from north to south. [*Toilers* I/vii/2].

Hugo knew fishermen at **Cobo** and made friends with some. He admired them. He observed a peculiarity that was a headache to census-makers trying to classify occupations –

> The fisherman farms, the market gardener sells fish; the same man is a labourer of the soil and a labourer of the sea [M xii/543].

Dally devotes pages to **Vazon Bay**; we have abbreviated his discussion. Hugo has a passing reference to the Corban –

> Si l'on creuse les alluvîons de la baie Vason, on y trouve des arbres. Il y a là, sous une mystérieuse épaisseur de sable, une forêt. [*If you dig the alluvial deposits of Vazon Bay, you find trees. There, beneath a mysterious thickness of sand, exists a forest.*] [M xii/517]

Hugo made frequent visits to the west coast. For personal reasons he incorporated two locations – the Marquand farm and '*mon île*.' These places were linked. Henri Marquand was one of Hugo's best friends in Guernsey. They met soon after Hugo's arrival and Marquand became a frequent guest at Hauteville House. As editor of *La Gazette de Guernesey* Marquand was well informed about local matters. He had a robust political stance – similar in its principles to those of Hugo. A friendship was almost inevitable. Marquand had a good understanding of agriculture and acquired a farm on the west coast at the **Mare de Carteret**.

On 23 October 1867 Victor Hugo recorded in his *Agenda* that he had paid 5 francs to his good friend M. Henry Marquand for the island that he had bought from him. [M xiii/1048]. The date is significant. Hugo had only recently returned from his holiday on the Continent. During his absence Marquand's daughter Emilie had died in tragic circumstances. At their farm, she ate some poisonous berries and died.

Emilie had been born in July 1864 and Hugo was her godfather. He chose for her the names Emilie-Adèle-Julie-Victorine. In July

1867 Emilie died shortly after her birthday, just three years old. Hugo grieved. In his *Agenda* he pasted a photograph and wrote *poor little Emily*. [M xiii/1045]. I suggest that Hugo's acquisition of the island on the west coast of Guernsey is linked to the tragic death of little Emilie.

There is some confirmation. On 6 July 1869 [M xiv/1432] Mme Marquand presented Hugo with a bouquet of 21 different flowers – some very sweet-smelling – that she had picked on his island near **Portinfer** (*Mme Marquand a cuelli dans mon île près Port-Enfer un bouquet de vingt et une fleurs différentes, quelques-unes très odorantes*). July was little Emilie's month – the month of her birth in 1864, the month of her death in 1867. Mme Marquand and Hugo were remembering Emilie. The island was important to Hugo, it was ever '*mon île*'. It connected him in symbolic fashion with the Marquand family in general, with his godchild in particular. Like Gilliatt, she had an isle; and the isle was her cenotaph.

There remains a mystery. Which island did Hugo buy? There are a few clues that I can offer.

1. On 16 June 1868 [*Agenda*] Hugo went on a tour to the west coast. He commented that he had seen the isle that he had bought from Marquand between 'Port Enfer et la maison Talbot.' [M xiv/1372].
2. On 15 May 1869 [*Agenda*] Hugo listed his itinerary as '…Port Enfer. mon île. la ferme de Carteret. les Grandes Rocques…' [M xiv/1418].
3. As we have already seen, Mme Marquand gathered flowers on the island. The island must have been
   a. easy of access to her and
   b. sufficiently fertile to support 21 different flowers

There are several islands between Portinfer and Grandes Rocques. Using the evidence of maps dating from 1787, 1938, and 1955, Ken Tough, for long Her Majesty's Greffier in Guernsey, has suggested that the relevant island was Le Noir Houmet. It seems to satisfy all the requirements. It is perhaps worth mentioning that Hugo does not make reference to Port Soif, the location of two candidate islands. Portinfer is repeatedly mentioned in the context of '*mon ile*'. Dinah Bott, a librarian at the Priaulx Library and chairman of the Victor Hugo in Guernsey Society, has conducted a thorough examination of documents dealing with the lands held by the Marquand family on the west coast of Guernsey. Her research suggests that there may not be documentary evidence for the island. The shifting sands of the littoral complicate the whole issue. She mentions that logically we should consider the possibility that the isle was in the Mare, not off the coast.

One final thought. In *les Travailleurs de la Mer* Gilliatt died at <u>Paradis</u> on the east coast of Guernsey. The tragic death of little Emilie was memorialised by Hugo at 'Port <u>Enfer</u>' on the west coast. The symmetry of the antonyms cannot have escaped Hugo's poetic intelligence.

Hugo regularly returned home *via* the **Talbot Valley**. He greatly admired it –

> Neither Tempe, Gémenos nor Val Suzon are more beautiful than the Vallée des Vaux in Jersey and Talbot Valley in Guernsey. [*L'Archipel* xvii].

Tempe in northern Greece was celebrated by poets as a favourite haunt of Apollo and the Muses. Gémenos in the south of France is surrounded by beautiful landscapes. Val Suzon in Burgundy was – and is – esteemed for its rich natural diversity. Hugo ranked the Guernsey valley alongside places of outstanding natural beauty in Classical antiquity, and in his beloved France. There could be no higher commendation.

Dally mentions three mills which gave **Kings Mills** its name – Moulin de Bas, Moulin du Milieu and Moulin de Haut. He overlooked a fourth mill – Moulin des Niaux (marked on the map and pictured on page 82). In Hugo's day it was inhabited by Jean Le Pelley (1789-1870) – an ancestor of the publisher of this monograph.

4: SOUTH WEST

EXCURSION 4

Câtel Church—Castle of Le Grand Jeffroi or Le Grand Sarazin—Fief d' Anville—Câtel Fair—Woodlands and its Picture Gallery—St. George—Cobo Church—St. Saviour's Parish—Union Hotel—Chapel of St. Appoline—Le Rée—Creux des Fées—Raised Beach—Rocquaine Bay—Lihou Island and Priory—Rock-pools—St. Saviour's Church—La Hougue Fouque.

On arriving from the Grange, at the end of the Rohais, ascend the road and hill on the left, which commands an extensive view of rich pasturage over all the northern part of the island, from Cobo and Grand Rock on the left, the Vale and L'Ancresse before you, and the Castle and St. Sampson on the extreme right, with the sea and the isle of Alderney in the distance. From no spot can the system of small holdings, caused by the frequent subdivision of property, be seen with such effect as from this. Two miles from the town is

Câtel Church,

or, the Church of "St. Mary of the Castle." Tradition reports, that long before the Conquest, on the site of the present church, stood the castle of one of the sea-kings, named "Le Grand Jeffroi," or "Le Grand Sarazin," whither he invited the pirates from the southern parts of France, bordering the Bay of Biscay, and bands of the northern freebooters, who aided him in piracy and pillage. A strong body of these marauders is said to have invaded this island in the year 1061, committing ravages upon the defenceless inhabitants, when Duke William of Normandy receiving information of the attack, despatched troops under command of Sampson D'Anville, who, landing at the harbour of St. Sampson, was joined by the monks and other inhabitants, who had sought refuge in the Castle of the Vale, and other places of retreat, defeated the invaders with much slaughter, killing or putting to flight *Le Grand Sarazin*, and levelling his stronghold with the ground. Duke William is reported to have made large grants of land in Guernsey to D'Anville, in reward of his valour. The present Fief D'Anville still attests this act of generosity : it is situate in the parish of St. Sampson, and is the noblest tenure in the island ; the *seigneur* ranks after the clergy, and is bound, when the king visits it, to attend him as his esquire. In commemoration of this conquest, the present church, built on the spot, was dedicated to "Our Lady of the Deliverance of the Castle ;" it was consecrated, with great pomp, on the 25th of August, 1203.

There are appearances in the north and east walls of the church, from which it has been inferred that they formed a part of the ancient *Castel du Grand Jeffroi* ; and some curious paintings in fresco, were discovered of late years, when the church was undergoing repairs.

The architecture of the church has but little to recommend it, though the clearance of the plaster from the arches dividing the aisle from the chancel, has exposed the warm-coloured granite, with a pleasing effect. It has a tower and northern transept. The nave is partitioned off, and forms a large interior vestibule on entering from the western porch. The Rev.—Carey is the incumbent.

This church, as did the castle of old, stands on an eminence nearly in the centre of the island, and commands an extensive view of the ocean, and of many of the landing-places : in the churchyard, amongst many tombs of old Guernsey families, is one of great interest, erected to the memory of ten poor mariners, who, on the 16th November, 1849, perished through shipwreck of the Barque "L'Europe" on the rocks off the *Homet D'Albec*, near Vazon Bay ; a rude attempt at sculpture portrays the catastrophe, and an appropriate epitaph records and laments their fate.

Câtel Fair

is really a *cattle* fair, held at Easter, Midsummer, and Michaelmas, on a plot of greensward about two hundred yards from the church. The show of island bulls, cows, and heifers, with a sprinkling of pigs, and latterly a few sheep, is well worth visiting.

The Agricultural Society, to which we have fully referred in another part, distributes prizes on these occasions. Passing through a little hamlet of farm-houses and cottages for a quarter of a mile, you will arrive at a gateway and carriage-drive, which leads to

Woodlands.

This is one of the most extensive and pretty estates in the island, the seat of Frederick Carey, Esq., a gentleman whose urbanity and kindness allow any respectable visitor to view it. The house has nothing particularly attractive in outward appearance, but *within* is the finest *collection of pictures* the island possesses. These, with great taste and judgment, have been selected by the proprietor during his travels in Spain, Italy, and elsewhere, and comprise many unique and valuable specimens of the old masters. The pleasure-grounds are beautifully undulating and romantic, at the extremity of which a door opening in the paddock-wall affords a truly picturesque view over Vazon Bay, King's Mills, and the adjacent country. There is a magnolia grandiflora of unusual height and size, growing near a well called the "Holy Well ;" and, indeed, all the rarer and more tender order of plants, which thrive so luxuriantly here, attest the mildness of the climate, and the advantages they derive from the shelter of this secluded spot.

We may now proceed to the foot of the hill to the cross roads, where there is a wayside seat commanding the view already described, when we brought the visitor from Cobo to this spot, and taking the road ascending to the right, he will, by a walk of less than half a mile, arrive at the estate called

St. George.

The beautiful grounds which surround this handsome country seat, tastefully planted with ornamental trees, are kindly open to the visits of strangers, and the hired carriage-driver, generally unsolicited, takes you through them. Here is also an ivied well, surmounted with a cross, called

"The Holy Well of St. George,"

to which tradition ascribed the power of showing anxious maidens the features of their future husbands. The maiden was then, it is said, entitled to claim the aid of the Church, if the youth proved unwilling.

The main road from *St. George* to the north, leads on to Saumarez, and thence to Cobo, as before described ; but, turning down the lane on the *left*, next the upper entrance gate of St. George's, and again, taking the *second* lane on your left hand, called *Haut Pavé*, you reach, in a walk of about a quarter of a mile,

Cobo Church.

This is a district, not a parish church, the nomination of the minister being vested in the rector of the Câtel : it is in the Norman style of architecture, of red-coloured granite from the adjoining quarries. It contains a chancel and vestry, nave and porch: the windows of the former are or stained glass, representing scenes from the life of the Saviour, and its floor is of encaustic tiles. The parsonage-house, built in corresponding style, is contiguous to the churchyard. Both these erections were at the cost of the Carey family, so numerous here, the endowment being raised by subscription. The present incumbent is the Rev.—Dobrée. This church was consecrated in 1854, and is dedicated to St. Matthew. There is an infant school near, supported by subscription, and another school for boys and girls in the immediate neighbourhood.

It should be observed, that the sittings in this little church are all free, and that thus both the spiritual and mental want a of the old and young, rich and poor, in a district afar from the parish church, and thickly tenanted by humble fishermen, of course with numerous offspring, are amply supplied.

Continuing his route past the church, the traveller will arrive in a few minutes at *Vazon Bay*, whence he may either make his detour through *King's Mills*, as before described, or proceed by the sea-side road, skirting the bay for about a mile, towards Richmond, where a barrack formerly stood, the houses of which have been let by the Government authorities to different tenants, some of whom make them their summer residences, the right being retained of re-entry in the event of war requiring their occupation by troops. This road leads into the

Parish of St. Saviour;

the church of which stands on the hill, about a mile and a half off. Another route to this is by St. Andrew's, as we shall have occasion to show in another walk or drive ; but this is by far the most accessible mode or reaching the lower and more interesting part of the parish. It will repay the tourist to ascend the hill, at the junction of the road with that from the King's Mills, to an eminence called "Le Mont Saint." The view is very picturesque. Descending the hill through the village, at a short distance he will espy a very comfortable inn—

The Union Hotel;

where he, or the horses, may by this time require rest and refreshment.

The next object worthy his attention, at a distance of two hundred yards hence, on the right-hand side of the road, is

The Chapel of St. Appoline.

This chapel is of great antiquity, and is the only one standing of the many similar ecclesiastical structures in use prior to the erection of the parish churches. The interior consists of a plain chamber, about 27 feet long by 14 feet 9 inches wide, having a narrow square-headed opening or loophole at the east end, a rude round-arched or segmental doorway, and a narrow window, divided into two parts, on the south side, and a smaller segmental doorway and window on the north side ; it is covered with a pointed and ponderous vaulted roof. The sides of the roof and walls appear to have been adorned with fresco paintings, several figures of saints being still discernible on the south wall. Nothing is known of the date when this building was erected, nor are there any traditional accounts of it among the inhabitants, but it is considered to be the oldest in Guernsey. The monks are reputed to have come to this island about the middle of the tenth century, and this, and its contemporary chapels, may therefore have been erected by them soon after their arrival, either for their own devotions, or before they had converted many to the faith, as the size of the chapel would not admit of more than about twenty persons. Architectural art must have been at a very low ebb, as will be seen by an inspection of the interior workmanship, especially that of the south window.

The silver-gilt chalice belonging to this chapel is still preserved, in the possession of Colonel Guille, round which are the words "Sancte Paule ora pro nobis," from which it may be inferred that the name of St. Appoline, "unknown to fame," is a corruption of St. Paul. It is deeply to be regretted that this relic of antiquity should have been so long suffered to fall into dilapidation: it is now used only as a barn, and is usually filled with dried fern and other fuel. A correspondent of the "Guernsey Star" very properly suggested its appropriation to a better purpose, by having it renovated and restored for the performance of divine service, in a spot so far distant from any church, where he (the writer) had no doubt many of the unbeneficed clergy would willingly give their gratuitous ministrations ; and if only the twenty which the chapel has been considered capable of accommodating assembled there, has it not been expressly promised that "where *two* or *three* are gathered together in His name, there will He be in the midst of them ?"

The road will now take us down by a walk of about half a mile to the promontory of *Le Rée*, where formerly were barracks, now appropriated, like those of Richmond, to more peaceful purposes. Near this spot, on the road leading to the little island of Lihou (afterwards described), is the far-famed

Creux des Fées

This so-called "Fairies' Cave" is a cromlech of more perfect character than many of the others, having been purchased by a gentleman to secure its preservation. It consists of two large cap-stones, which measure about twenty feet across, covering a considerable-sized chamber, and supported by numerous props. The opening is from the east; but it is dark and gloomy within from the interstices between the props being stopped with earth and stones.

There are evidences of there having been other Celtic remains in this neighbourhood, and within half a mile is another small cromlech belonging to the same gentleman : it stands on the hill of *Catioroc*, and may be found by asking the peasants for "Le Trepied." It consists of three or four stones : burnt bones, with portions of urns and pottery, have been exhumed from beneath it. Near the causeway which leads to Lihou there are appearances of a "raised beach," interesting to the geologist, as evidence that the level of these islands has been in different ages materially altered by powers of elevation or depression at work in the interior of our planet. The district about Lihou, probably the island itself, was at a remote period at a much lower elevation than at present ; afterwards it seems to have become raised above its present level, and a gradual process of subsidence appears to be now taking place.

The Bay of Rocquaine

comes next under notice, bounded at the southern extremity by a
point of land and Fort Grey, with the rocky heights of Pleinmont,
and towards the north by the headland of Le Rée, guarded by
Saumarez Fort, whence is a causeway leading to

The Island and Priory of Lihou.

This spot, the extreme western point of the island, situate about
six miles from the town, is only accessible at half-tide; neither is it
advisable to visit it when the sea is coming in, unless you intend to
prolong your stay for some hours.

There formerly stood a priory and chapel here, but the ruins
of the latter only now attest the existence of this monastic retreat,
which by reason of its lonely and secluded situation, became the
chosen abode of a prior, or, as some allege, of an abbess and her
nuns. Such a character for sanctity did the island acquire, that it is
said that the French coasters are in the habit, even in the present
day, of saluting it when passing by lowering their topmasts. The date
of the erection of the priory and chapel is unknown : though it was,
no doubt, the retreat of the monks long before the consecration
of the chapel, which, according to the *Dédicace des Eglises*, took
place in 1114, three years later than that of the earliest church in
Guernsey—St. Sampson's ; it was dedicated to the Virgin Mary.

Towards the close of the last century the chapel was entire as
regards the walls and roof, the ornamental parts, which were of Caen
stone, alone being mutilated. During the last war with France the
lieutenant-governor, fearing lest the building might be turned into
some use by the enemy, ordered its complete demolition, which was
effected by means of gunpowder. Subsequent excavations, however,
have brought to light many of the details, the chapel forming the
most prominent feature. It consists of a chancel and nave, with a
square tower on the north-east side of the nave. It was vaulted with

stone; and the north wall of the nave, with a few feet of the roof, is still standing. The excavations in the chancel disclosed the debris of the walls and roof, with the Caen-stone ribs of the groined roof, and the stones which formed the columns and the windows : at a depth of four feet a pavement of small green and red glazed Norman tiles was discovered, with which the whole appears to have been paved, and below this were found a few monastic coins and some silver pennies of Edward I.

In no spot around Guernsey can the rock-pools, so interesting to the naturalist, be seen to better advantage than among the rocky barriers of this little island of Lihou. On the south-east side, at about half-water mark, where a vein of felspar traverses the gneiss, are two almost circular excavations in the rock, formed apparently by the action of the strong currents and the friction of the stones hurled against the cliffs, on this exposed side of the Bay of Rocquaine. Fiction has given them the name of baths, for which their form and depth, of from four to five feet with a shelving bottom, singularly adapts them ; and tradition asserts that they were used for this purpose by the nuns of the priory. One is formed a little above the other, the water of the upper dripping over a ledge into the lower one, while a rounded lip carries off the water from the latter, leaving both pools full nearly to the brim. These pools, though diminutive in size, afford ample amusement and instruction as long as the tide will allow an inspection of them. "Their beautiful lining of corallines and sponges, with many minute and rosy algæ ; their pellucid and motionless waters, slightly tinged with blue ; their animated occupants—tiny molluscs and crustaceans, the one in leisurely movements, the other darting among the sea-weeds, presented a picture of a microcosm—a world in little, such as only a rock-pool can display." (Rambles among the Channel Islands: by a Naturalist).

We will now suppose our visitor returned to the main land, and surveying the beauties of *Rocquaine Bay* : but at no time can its grandeur be so fully appreciated as during the prevalence of a storm with a gale from the south-west—its most turbulent quarter—

when the waves rush, impeded only by reefs of rocks, direct from the Atlantic, raging and thundering on the shore, uplifting huge masses of granite from their foundations, and completely concealing from your view with sea-foam and spray the little island of Lihou we have just quitted.

In a field next the road, towards the centre of this bay, called Catillon, stands a rock, having the semblance of the impression caused by two human feet, supposed to mark the boundary between the two former chapelries of Lihou and St. Brioc, and near which, in 1829, a quantity of coins, amounting to near seven hundred in number, were dug up. The greater part were silver pennies, a few copper, of the reigns of Philip IV. of France, and Edward II. of England.

As we have now taken a long day's excursion, we recommend the visitor to return by the same road, and through King's Mills, to the town, unless he prefers the longer route, which leads past the little school at Le Rée, through the parishes of St. Peter in the Wood and the Forest (whither we purpose conducting him another day), and thence through St. Martin's ; or, the traveller may prefer a change of scenery, and return through St. Saviour's by taking the turn to the right, a short distance beyond the *Union Hotel*, and ascending the hill beyond the late Alexander's tavern, by the parish school, towards St. Saviour's Church.

This stands on an elevated spot, with an extensive view, and overlooks a wooded valley below ; there are some pretty walks in the neighbourhood, particularly by the narrow lane descending westward of the church, through rural hamlets and undulating scenery.

The church is of the simplest style of Gothic architecture, built in 1154, and has nothing worthy of notice within or without. Not far from this is an elevation of ancient date, called

La Hougue Fouque.

There are several of these mounds in various parts of the island ; their use in early ages was for watch-towers, on which were kindled beacons to warn the inhabitants of the approach of pirates, or of any hostile fleet.

The high road hence, by a very tortuous course, leads through the pretty village of St. Andrew, via Mount Row, to the town, a distance of about four miles.

L'Erée & Lihou Island, Guernsey.

Above: L'Erée & Lihou Island
Below: Country Scene (Henry Wimbush)

Above: St Appoline (Joshua Gosselin, Guernsey Museum & Art Gallery)
Below: St George's Well

Above: Guernsey woman gathering fuel
Below: Le Creux des Fées (Lukis Collection; Kendrick p.187)

Above: Milkmaids
Below: Country Scene

EXCURSION 4: COMMENTARY

Hugo frequently made forays into this area. He was amused by the natural history of **Lihou** –

> Lihou is a small island just off the coast, uninhabited, accessible at low tide. It is covered in scrub and burrows. The rabbits of Lihou are conscious of the time of day. They only come out of their holes at high tide. They defy man and mock him. Their friend the ocean keeps them isolated. Great affinities of this kind are what nature is all about. [M xii/517].

Câtel Fair – Hugo visited the *marché aux bestiaux* on several occasions. It was situated at what today is called Fairfield – on the corner of Route de l'Eglise and Rue de la Foire, not far from Castel Church.

Hugo took a lively interest in farming. In *L'Archipel* he commented -

> Terre fertile, grasse, forte. Nul pâturage meilleur. Le froment est célèbre, les vaches sont illustres. Les génisses des herbages de Saint-Pierre-du-Bois sont les égales des moutons lauréats du plateau de Confolens. [M xii/516].

> *Fertile, rich, strong soil. No better pasturage. The wheat is celebrated, the cows are famous. The heifers from the grass of St Peter-in-the-Wood are the equal of the prized sheep of the plateau of Confolens.*

The folklore of **St George** interested him –

> Girls can see the reflection of the man they will marry in St George's spring in Câtel parish. [M xii/541].

Hugo sometimes refers to a haunted house on the road between Forest and St Saviour. [M xiv/1368]. He was fascinated by such houses.

Commenting on Gilliatt's house, he wrote –

In the islands of Jersey and Guernsey, sometimes in the country, but often in streets with many inhabitants, you will come upon a house the entrance to which is completely barricaded. Holly bushes obstruct the doorway, hideous boards, with nails, conceal the windows below; while the casements of the upper stories are neither closed nor open: for all the window-frames are barred, but the glass is broken. If there is a little yard, grass grows between its stones; and the parapet of its wall is crumbling away. If there is a garden, it is choked with nettles, brambles, and hemlock, and strange insects abound in it. The chimneys are cracked, the roof is falling in; so much as can be seen from without of the rooms presents a dismantled appearance. The woodwork is rotten; the stone mildewed. The paper of the walls has dropped away and hangs loose, until it presents a history of the bygone fashions of paper-hangings—the scrawling patterns of the time of the Empire, the crescent-shaped draperies of the Directory, the balustrades and pillars of the days of Louis XVI. The thick draperies of cobwebs, filled with flies, indicate the quiet reign long enjoyed by innumerable spiders. Sometimes a broken jug may be noticed on a shelf. Such houses are considered to be haunted. Satan is popularly believed to visit them by night. Houses are like the human beings who inhabit them. They become to their former selves what the corpse is to the living body. A superstitious belief among the people is sufficient to reduce them to this state of death. Then their aspect is terrible. These ghostly houses are common in the Channel Islands. [*Toilers* I/i/2].

5: SOUTH COAST & THE HAUNTED HOUSE

EXCURSION 5

Road to St. Andrew—The Bailiff's Cross—St. Andrew's Church—The Parish of The Forest—Petit-Bôt Bay—La Moie Point—Le Gouffre—La Corbière—Le Havre de Bon Repos—Torteval Church—Creux Mahié—Pleinmont—Shipwrecks—The Congerel—Les Thielles—St. Peter's in the Wood—The Church—Meulier, or Pillar of Stone—Different Roads and distances back to the Town.

We now vary our route through St. Andrew's. The road to this little inland village, the only parish that is not in some part bounded by the sea, is by way of the Grange, Queen's Road, and Mount Row; proceeding thence, at the foot of the hill on your left hand lies *Vauquiédor*, the seat of J. Le Mottee, Esq., one of the jurats ; and on the left *Havilland Hall*, for some years past the residence of the lieutenant-governor. Ascending the hill, you arrive at a *carrefour*, or four cross roads, a mile from the town, called—

The Bailiff's Cross.

The tale connected with this belongs rather to romance than history, but it is related in all the Guernsey histories, and is generally credited.

One Gaultier de la Salle, who stands on the list of bailiffs of the island in 1284, resided on his estate, then called "La Petite Ville," about half a mile hence, had a poor neighbour, named Massey, who was proprietor of a cottage, with a little land, near the bailiff's, and had a right of drawing water from a well on the premises of the latter. The exercise of this right being an annoyance to the bailiff, he sought to become the purchaser of Massey's land, or otherwise to dispossess his troublesome neighbour ; and failing in all his attempts, he resorted to a diabolical scheme for gratifying his revenge.

In order to accomplish this he concealed two silver cups in one of his own corn-ricks, and suborning witnesses to convict poor Massey of the theft, he caused him to be arrested and brought to trial, when he was found guilty.

On the morning of the trial the bailiff had directed his men to remove into his barn a particular rick, which he *distinctly* pointed out to them, and then left his home to assume his office of judge with his brother jurats, a second Judas among the twelve. It happened that the men fortunately mistook their master's orders, and set to work at the other rick, in which they shortly discovered the missing plate.

At the moment when sentence of death was being passed on poor Massey, one of the men, who had hurried with all his speed, rushed breathlessly into court, holding up the cups, and calling out, "They are found ! they are found !"

The bailiff, thrown off his guard, passionately rising, exclaimed, "Thou fool ! *that* was not the rick I told you to remove : I knew – ".

Here he sank into his seat, with a countenance betraying a guilty conscience, and a dead pause ensued throughout the court.

The jurats consulted for a while, when Massey was set at liberty; and after a short trial, De la Salle was convicted of "feloniously compassing the death of an innocent man," and was sentenced to the ignominious end he had planned for his victim.

It is said that on his way to execution he stopped at this spot to receive the sacrament ; from which circumstance it derives its name to this day of *Le Croix au Bailiff*, or Bailiffs Cross, still denoted by a stone having a X rudely cut upon it, now nearly imbedded in the earth.

The bailiff's estate being forfeited to the Crown, received the name it still bears of "La Ville au Roi," and is subject to a feudal service. Whenever the Cour St. Michel holds a *chevauchée*, the owner is bound by his tenure to furnish the *peons*, or esquires, with sweet milk ; and in 1825, when the last procession took place, the members halted opposite the estate, and milk was abundantly supplied to them in a silver cup. This old house stands on the road leading from Mount Row to St. Martin : until last year it formed a very interesting ruin ; but the picturesque gable and roof, and the remaining arch of the gateway becoming dilapidated, it was considered so unsafe as to require demolition, though enough remains in the granite sculptured doorway, and space for armorial shield above, with the turreted spiral stair, and some ivy-clad outhouses, to make the spot an interesting relic of the olden time.

The Bailiff's Cross Road leads direct to Câtel Church ; the first turning on the right runs through a valley skirted with substantial farm-houses to the Foulon ; that on the left, by a pleasant walk, to the Talbot Road, or to St. Andrew's. Further on this road to Câtel, another lane (neither of the three exceeding a mile) will take you by its devious way down to the old water-mill, called *Le Moulin de l'Echelle*, from the circumstance that the miller was by his tenure bound to do "suit and service" in providing the ladder used at the executions, which took place at the four cross roads above named; in fact, the whole country hereabouts is intersected by rural lanes running through valleys "with verdure clad," and affording glimpses of inland beauty that no highway can afford.

We now again start from the Bailiff's Cross by the straight road from the town, and at a distance of two miles thence arrive at

St. Andrew's Church.

This is by far the most picturesque and perfectly rural church in the whole island, peculiarly resembling one of our English village shrines ; by-the-by, "the earliest violets," of which this churchyard is stated by a fanciful female historian to boast, must have been planted there by some fair fingers from the rectory, for everyone is conscious of the fact, a very extraordinary one, that not a single scented violet, blue or white, grows in a wild state in Guernsey, those poor pale blue semblances which deck the hedgerows being only the common scentless dog-violet of our English woods.

This pretty church is a Gothic building, flanked with buttresses, having a castellated tower and spire at the west, with the here unusual but convenient accompaniment of a clock. The parsonage house is close to it : the Rev. R. J. Ozanne is the rector. The contiguity of this church to the town, and the pleasant walk to it, renders it available to many English, who attend on the alternate Sunday mornings and afternoons, when the service is in English. The seats are free.

On the left, a hundred yards hence, stands the *Manor House of St. Helena*, the residence of John Carey, Esq., and a little further on the road, on your right hand, is the estate called *Vaubellets*, the property of the Mansell family. At the end of this, skirted by a little wayside inn, there stood one of the most beautifully-shaded avenues in the island, now replaced by a stone wall. Proceeding by this through what remains of the avenue at the end and continuing till you have passed a little dissenting chapel embosomed in trees, three roads meet, the right hand leading to the forest, the two other to St. Saviour.

Either the road above named, or that from the Vaubellets, will conduct the tourist in less than a mile to the parish of *La Forêt*, or

The Forest.

The approach to this village by the road from St. Martin's is so dull and devoid of interest that we have preferred bringing our visitor by this not much more circuitous route ; he may reach *Petit-Bôt Bay*, its chief attraction, by turning off at the road next the post-office at St. Martin's, and then taking the next lane on the right ; but the best and most imposing approach to it is by the road to the left of the Forest Church.

Petit-Bôt Bay.

This, as its name imports, is the tiniest as well as one of the most beautiful of all these interesting inlets. The bay opens into the sea at the termination of a narrow glen from either side, whether you approach it from the east or west, one of the sides of which is formed of abrupt and uneven rocks. A little stream sparkles down the ravine, dances among the pebbles of the upper part of the beach, and then disappears, except at low water, when it again forces its bright way through the sands in narrow rivulets, and then loses itself in the sea. A water-mill, half hidden in trees, and a house beside it, where refreshments can be had, and parties of pleasure accommodated, stands facing the bay, which is guarded by a martello-tower.

Some of the rocks forming the sides of this bay have a peculiarly grand appearance. Their sides are vertical, and they plunge without a break into the pure and transparent water, their hard outlines being distinctly visible below the surface. There is a cave extending to a small depth in the rock at the side of this bay where the beautiful fern *Asplenium marinum* grows in great perfection; but the ravages of collectors have made it rare, and they must have scaled the walls of this cave to reach it.

The scenery on either side of the bay is extremely fine ; the bold outlines of the rocks at Moulin Houet, with the fantastic architecture of those nearer at hand, and the blue stretch of the water filling every creek, and adapting itself to all the ruggedness of the coast-line, form a picture composed of beautiful elements, producing an exquisite effect.

To enjoy the scene in perfection the visitor should ascend the hills on either side of the bay. That on the right, facing the sea, is not easily accessible, except by rugged sheep-tracks ; but to the left is a pathway which will well repay the pains taken to mount it. If the pedestrian is in earnest, he will also take the "right path," whence, as if "among the fragments of a world upturned," his eye will wander over wild chasms and dazzling precipices, the waves of the sea miniatured beneath, and the noise of their waters hushed by distance. After rambling another mile, he reaches

La Moie Point.

There is a road from the Forest Church by which a carriage can descend a considerable part of the way to a cottage standing at a turn of the road, where a horse or two can be stabled or stalled. But by far the best approach to every bay and scene of beauty on this side the island is on foot, through devious and delightful lanes. One of these leads to the point of land, or, rather, of rock, named above, the scenery from which is of a most commanding aspect. Eastward of this promontory is a tiny harbour, affording anchorage for a few fishing-smacks, which look like toy-boats, in the waters at your very feet.

Another pathway, leading from the cottage just mentioned, conducts immediately down to

Le Gouffre.

This appropriately-named abyss is at the extremity of a narrow gorge, between the lofty precipices of which a babbling stream pursues its silvery way. The scenery is grand, the solitude most impressive ; the little rivulet, freshening a pathway of the greenest turf, flows in a slender thread over the tall cliff, down into the surging billows, losing its music in the roar of the ocean. Nature seems to have left nothing undone in this sequestered spot. There is a green sward ready prepared whereon to sit, "eat, drink, and be merry," if you have advisedly brought a supply of "creature comforts " in your wallet ; or, if not, she offers you a refreshing draught from the brook, and food for the mind in the contemplation of her miracles around. Listen to her voice in that roaring gulf, and feel grateful for her health-giving breath in those genial breezes from the sea, and then must your heart echo back the inspired apostrophe of the Psalmist, "O Lord, how wonderful are thy works ! in wisdom hast thou made them all !"

La Corbière

is another promontory on a smaller scale than La Moie. The more adventurous pedestrian may reach it by way of the cliffs westward of the Gouffre, or more inland, through the furze-lined lanes. There seem to be some remains of the fosse and mound of what is reported to have been an ancient fortress, guarding this point and the neighbouring little bay called

Le Havre de Bon Repos

so well deserving its name for its quiet solitude—a fitting place of rest on a calm sunny day, after climbing the wild crags that everywhere surround it. At most times during the summer a boat may be hired here with an experienced fisherman to take you to the neighbouring cave, which we shall describe presently.

We have now entered the parish of Torteval bounded by the cliffs on the south and extreme south-west point of the island, and situate among the boldest and wildest of its rocky scenery. Unless the stranger has reached the lower part of this parish and its church by the lanes, being attracted by the obelisk-like structure before him, he may arrive at

Torteval Church,

by a road leading to the left, and two miles distant from the Forest Church. Built of cold blue granite, and of the most formal design, it evinces the want of architectural taste prevailing here so lately as 1818, when it was completed and consecrated ; more especially when we find this the last parish church built in the island, replacing one fallen into decay, and described as having "a chancel, nave, south aisle, and porch, and a low, square tower, pinnacled, and surmounted by an octagonal spire." Tradition tells us that a certain Philip de Carteret, of the Jersey family of that name, so famous during the Commonwealth as stanch adherents of King Charles, while encountering a violent storm at sea off this shore, made a vow that if Providence spared his life, he would found a church on the first land he reached in safety. By almost a miracle, considering the rocky shore, the vessel made the harbour in Rocquaine bay in the middle of the night, and De Carteret performed his vow by building or endowing this church in 1229 or 1230. That such was not the original church, however, is apparent from an early charter in 1055, more than ten years before the Conquest, in which the old church is mentioned as "ecclesia Sancti Marie de Tortavalle." Another curious circumstance connected with the present church is, that Dr. Fisher, Bishop of Salisbury, acting for the Bishop of Winchester, who was incapacitated through age and infirmities from crossing the Channel, consecrated this church in 1818, and was the first Protestant Bishop that ever landed in the Channel Islands. He came in the "Tiber," a 46-gun frigate, and at the same time consecrated the new church of St. James in the town.

Within half a mile of the church is

The Creux Mahié

This remarkable cave is situate on the south side of this parish, at the head of a small creek, and is the most considerable cavern, in point of size, in Guernsey. It appears to have been formed by the action of the waves wearing away the softer portions of the rock to an extent of about two hundred feet in depth and forty to fifty in width, its height varying from twenty to sixty feet. At some distant period a huge block of the cliff above the cave has fallen, partially blocking up the entrance, and forming a sort of terrace, which keeps off the sea ; but the opening is thus so much reduced as to be difficult to discover until close beside it, as you descend the rude steps leading down from this terrace.

The effect is very fine as soon as the eye becomes accustomed to the imperfect light, or it is best seen to advantage by exploring it with lights, or illuminating it by means of bundles of furze that may be obtained at the neighbouring cottages, and which, when ignited, throw the lofty dome-shaped vault and the masses of detached rock into strong lights and shadows, and wild and fantastic shapes, presenting a striking and impressive scene ; while a feeling of mystery is excited by smaller caves and fissures in the walls of the cavern, which, though easily traced to their termination, are confidently asserted by the peasantry to lead deep into the bowels of the earth, even to the centre of the island. The same tale, with quite as little truth, is told in our account of another cave, the *Creux des Fées*. The tourist must now retrace his steps towards Torteval Church, whence, by rather a rough road for Guernsey, where they are generally excellent, he will reach in a ramble of a mile the rocky heights of

Pleinmont.

This is the great attraction for the meeting of picnic parties and the lovers of the grand and the beautiful in nature. There is a farm-house within about a mile of the spot, which itself must be visited on foot, or those lofty and otherwise inaccessible cliffs to the south, branching eastward of a ruined guard-house, easily discernible, can never be gained even a sight of. To the west, extending nearly two miles, is the dangerous reef of rocks called Les Hanois, on which many a good ship has gone to pieces. In 1808, H. M. S. "Boreas," shortly after leaving St. Peter Port, in fine, calm weather, was wrecked here, and but few of her crew were saved. It has been long in contemplation to erect a lighthouse on or near these rocks; and that "consummation, so devoutly to be wished," is now about to be realized. After many disputes who should be the contributors to the cost of so vast an undertaking, the burthen of which was attempted to be thrown on the islanders, Government has undertaken it, and under direction of the Trinity House, workshops on a large scale are erected on the south pier at Guernsey, where the stone is worked and conveyed in barges to the spot, and it is expected that within three years the lighthouse will be completed. Although these rocks are now nearly covered at high tide, there is evidence to show that at a former period they must have been connected with the mainland. Traces of roads are said to be discernible at very low tides, and an order, of ancient date, for their repair is reported to be still extant. These Hanois Rocks, the *raised* beach near the adjacent island of Lihou, and the *submerged* forest of Vazon Bay, afford contrary, though contiguous, phenomena, interesting to the geologist as examples of changes which have occurred in the relative elevation of the land and water.

At the spot called the *Gouffre*, and another westward called the *Bigard*, and all around Pleinmont, the rocks assume their greatest degree of wild and confused arrangement. Their hardness of outline is particularly visible at these places, and the almost adamantine resistance they offer to the incessant buffetings of the sea, tends to preserve this character. Lichens of various hues, green, golden, and white, clothe the higher parts of the rocks, and communicate to them a solemn and ancient look. Clusters of samphire here and there rest upon the narrow ledges, and look green and fresh by the side of the apparently juiceless and withered vegetation which enwraps the sur face of the cliffs. The sea-gull dwells in the inaccessible heights, and sea-fowl scream over the boisterous waste below. The wind, bearing clouds of vapour from the bosom of the warm Atlantic, often clothes their summits with white, while the heavy surf also shrouds in white their wave-washed base.

A continued succession of similar scenes, yet each diverse from the other, presents itself to the termination of this coast, on this side the island. One rock, in particular, attracts notice from its isolated position in the water ; and from the peculiar boldness of outline which it exhibits it is called the *Congerel*. It can only be reached by means of a boat, and its solitude is consequently seldom invaded by any creatures other than the sea-birds, which make it their abode. At Pleinmont, where the rocks receive the full force of the Atlantic storms, some interesting effects of their action on the rocks are observable. At the point to the eastward, called *Les Thielles*, the intrusion of veins of trap into the gneiss rocks gives a new feature to the latter. The lines of dark veins strongly contrast with the colour of the gneiss, and something of the step or terrace like appearance, peculiar to rocks thus constituted, be comes visible. In some places the intruding veins are as thin as the edge of a knife, in others they are some feet in breadth.

We will now return through the pretty village and parish of

St. Peter in the Wood,

which brings back our memories and gladdens our hearts with a faithful resemblance of our village green, and its Gothic church— this sacred edifice being the best and most perfect of its kind throughout the island. It consists of a chancel and nave, north and south aisles, and square battlemented tower. The windows are richly decorated with tracery, some of which were dilapidated, having been restored in the same style of architecture. How it obtained, or if it ever deserved the name of *St. Pierre du Bois*, we know not, as no vestige of a wood is to be seen.

Here, as in every other parish, is the parochial school, and there is an infant school which we before pointed out near Le Rée, with suitable teachers, under the superintendence of the Rev. Carey Brock, the rector. There are two roads in the vicinity of the church leading to each extremity of the Bay of Rocquaine ; one has most probably brought our traveller hither ; the other, the main military road, leads to Le Rée and Lihou ; on the left-hand side of this road, in a field belonging to the estate of *Les Paysans*, stands

A Pillar of Stone, or Menhir.

The imposing position of this relic of antiquity has attracted the attention, and in vain raised the curiosity of the natives, who have held it in a sort of veneration, and have, of course, invested it with fictitious interest and fairy visitings. Whether it is an idolatrous altar, or pillar dedicated to the Deity, or cenotaph, or Celtic remain, is unknown either from tradition or history. It stands about ten feet above the surface of the ground, and is about three feet in width, and there it has stood, perhaps, for more than two thousand years, puzzling, and to puzzle, the brains of the antiquarian.

The visitor may now return to the town by *this* road, a distance of about six miles through the King's Mills, or retrace his path by way of St. Peter in the Wood, the Forest, and Saint Martin's, which is not more than five miles, but the former is the most pleasant, as it will bear an oft-repeated visit. We have endeavoured to leave "no stone unturned," no road untraced ; but there are many more which the wanderer through the beauties of this island can only find for himself, none of which will fail to afford gratification and delight.

We have now, by dint of our own experience, accompanied the visitor to those points of the island most worthy of attention; and we have endeavoured to cull such details and descriptions of historical or local interest, as would best tend to illustrate each scene, and enliven the path of the stranger.

Water Mill, Petit Bôt (Henry Wimbush)

'Port au Quatrième Étage', Les Travailleurs de la Mer

La Moye Point today (photo: Adrian Bott)

Above: Le Gouffre village. Below: Le Gouffre Hotel.
Hugo and his guests dined here in July 1870 [M xiv/1492].

Le Gouffre Guernsey.

JWS 454

Above: Rocquaine Bay
Below: Torteval Church

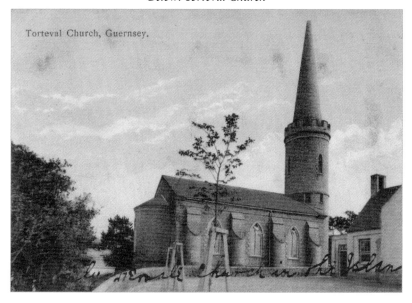

'La Maison Hantée, Pleinmont', Les Travailleurs de la Mer
Opposite: Maritime Map showing Les Hanois, Pleinmont
and the rocks mentioned by Hugo (see page 138).

Above: Victor Hugo's Haunted House, postcard (T.B. Banks)
The house was destroyed during the German occupation (1940-45),
but the lintel stone (below) was preserved
and is now in the Guernsey Museum.
(Guernsey Museum & Art Gallery)

Victor Hugo, Plainmont, la maison visionée
(Bibliothèque nationale de France,
N° d'inventaire NAF 24745 folio 123)

Les Hanois Lighthouse

Excursion 5: Commentary

This is a long excursion. Dally begins his chapter with the narration of a famous Guernsey story about a wicked bailiff. The story was known to Hugo. On 29 April 1869 he recorded that the bailiff committed the crime at Ville au Roi and expiated it at **Bailiff's Cross**. On 6 July 1869 he noted that they followed the way taken by the bailiff on his journey to execution. [M xiv/1414; 1432].

Hugo had come to know the south coast well by 1865, describing locations with precision in *The Toilers of the Sea* – La Moie Point, Torteval Church, Pleinmont, Hanois. Hugo had walked the territory. His brother-in-law Paul Chenay joined in one such expedition. He recounted Hugo's discovery of **La Moie**.

> The island of Guernsey is surrounded by high cliffs and promontories. On one of the highest of these cliffs, Victor Hugo had discovered in the course of one of his excursions a group of fishermen living with their families in a fairly comfortable community. The women and children looked after the cottages while the men were at sea. Every evening the catch and equipment would be hauled up to the top of the cliffs by means of ropes and hoists operated by all the members of the community who would gather as soon as the return of the boats was signalled by the man whose turn it was to be on watch.
>
> Without theorising and quite simply – isn't this the true implementation of mutuality and fraternity ...
>
> The joint efforts of these courageous people put the boats into shelter away from the fury of the waves, which would otherwise have smashed and scattered them had they been left exposed on these beaches bristling with dangers.
>
> Victor Hugo gave this fishermen's hamlet the name of le port

au quatrième étage. [Chenay, pp.235-6.]

Hugo incorporated this location in *The Toilers of the Sea*, making it the haunt of smugglers.

> On the southern coast of Guernsey behind Pleinmont, in the curve of a bay composed entirely of precipices and rocky walls rising peak-shaped from the sea, there is a singular landing-place, to which a French gentleman, a resident of the island since 1855, has given the name of "The Port on the Fourth Floor," a name now generally adopted. This port, or landing-place, which was then called the Moie, is a rocky plateau half-formed by nature, half by art, raised about forty feet above the level of the waves, and communicating with the water by two large beams laid parallel in the form of an inclined plane. The fishing-vessels are hoisted up there by chains and pulleys from the sea, and are let down again in the same way along these beams, which are like two rails. For the fishermen there is a ladder. The port was, at the time of our story, much frequented by the smugglers. Being difficult of access, it was well suited to their purposes. [*Toilers* I/vii/2].

Hugo briefly refers to **Torteval church** in *The Toilers of the Sea* –

> Three o'clock had sounded in the steeple of Torteval which is round and pointed like a magician's hat. [*Toilers* I/v/5].

Contemporaries were critical – Torteval did not sound the hours but, as Henri Marquand pointed out, a novelist is allowed some licence in his fiction. [Cox *Perspectives*, p.69].

Hugo visited **Pleinmont** on 19 June 1859 [M x/1531-2], soon after his return from the Sark holiday. Just as Sark inspired ideas that were to blossom in *The Toilers of the Sea*, so did Pleinmont. He jotted down notes about the *haunted house ... the house of Death*, and recorded the lintel inscription. The building became a tourist attraction in the late 19th century. English visitors were keen to view locations of the popular novel. The house was demolished by the German army during the Occupation years (1940-1945). Today only the foundations remain. Happily the lintel survived the attention of the Wehrmacht and it is now to be found in Candie Museum (see page 128). To return to Hugo –

> Pleinmont, near Torteval, is one of the three corners of the island of Guernsey. At the extremity of the cape there rises a high turfy hill, which looks over the sea.
>
> The height is a lonely place. All the more lonely from there being one solitary house there.
>
> This house adds a sense of terror to that of solitude.
>
> It is popularly believed to be haunted.
>
> Haunted or not, its aspect is singular.
>
> Built of granite, and rising only one story high, it stands in the midst of the grassy solitude. It is in a perfectly good condition as far as exterior is concerned; the walls are thick and the roof is sound. Not a stone is wanting in the sides, not a tile upon the roof. A brick-built chimney-stack forms the angle of the roof. The building turns its back to the sea, being on that side merely a blank wall. On examining this wall, however, attentively, the visitor perceives a little window bricked up. The two gables have three dormer windows, one fronting the east, the others fronting the west, but both are bricked up in like manner. The front, which looks inland, has alone a door and windows. This door, too, is walled in, as are also the two windows of the ground-floor. On the first floor—and this is the feature which is most striking as you approach—there are two open windows; but these are even more suspicious than the blind windows. Their open squares

look dark even in broad day, for they have no panes of glass, or even window-frames. They open simply upon the dusk within. They strike the imagination like hollow eye-sockets in a human face. Inside all is deserted. Through the gaping casements you may mark the ruin within. No panellings, no woodwork; all bare stone. It is like a windowed sepulchre, giving liberty to the spectres to look out upon the daylight world. The rains sap the foundations on the seaward side. A few nettles, shaken by the breeze, flourish in the lower part of the walls. Far around the horizon there is no other human habitation. The house is a void; the abode of silence: but if you place your ear against the wall and listen, you may distinguish a confused noise now and then, like the flutter of wings. Over the walled door, upon the stone which forms its architrave, are sculptured these letters, 'ELM-PBILG', with the date '1780'.

The dark shadow of night and the mournful light of the moon find entrance there.

The sea completely surrounds the house. Its situation is magnificent; but for that reason its aspect is more sinister. The beauty of the spot becomes a puzzle. Why does not a human family take up its abode here? The place is beautiful, the house well-built. Whence this neglect? To these questions, obvious to the reason, succeed others, suggested by the reverie which the place inspires. Why is this cultivatable garden uncultivated? No master for it; and the bricked-up doorway? What has happened to the place? Why is it shunned by men? What business is done here? If none, why is there no one here? Is it only when all the rest of the world are asleep that some one in this spot is awake? Dark squalls, wild winds, birds of prey, strange creatures, unknown forms, present themselves to the mind, and connect themselves somehow with this deserted house. For what class of wayfarers can this be the hostelry? You imagine to yourself whirlwinds of rain and hail beating in at the open casements, and wandering through the rooms. Tempests have left their vague traces upon the interior walls. The chambers, though walled and covered in, are visited by the hurricanes. Has the house been the scene of some great crime? You may almost fancy that this spectral dwelling, given up to solitude and darkness, might be heard calling aloud for succour. Does it remain silent? Do voices indeed issue from it? What business has it on hand in this lonely place? The mystery of the dark hours rests securely here. Its aspect is disquieting at noonday; what must it be at midnight? The dreamer asks himself—for dreams have their coherence—what this house may be between the dusk of evening and the twilight of approaching dawn? Has the vast supernatural world some relation with this deserted height, which sometimes compels it to arrest its movements here, and to descend and to become visible? Do the scattered elements of the spirit world whirl around it? Does the impalpable take form and substance here? Insoluble riddles! A holy awe is in the very stones; that dim twilight has surely relations with the infinite Unknown. When the sun has gone down, the song of the birds will be hushed, the goatherd behind the hills will go homeward with his goats; reptiles, taking courage from the gathering darkness, will creep through the fissures of rocks; the stars will begin to appear, night will come, but yonder two blank casements will still be staring at the sky. They open to welcome spirits and apparitions; for it is by the names of apparitions, ghosts, phantom faces vaguely distinct, masks in the lurid light, mysterious movements of minds, and shadows, that the popular faith, at once ignorant and profound, translates the sombre relations of this dwelling with the world of darkness.

The house is 'haunted' the popular phrase comprises everything.

Credulous minds have their explanation; common-sense

thinkers have theirs also. 'Nothing is more simple,' say the latter, 'than the history of the house. It is an old observatory of the time of the revolutionary wars and the days of smuggling. It was built for such objects. The wars being ended, the house was abandoned; but it was not pulled down, as it might one day again become useful. The door and windows have been walled to prevent people entering, or doing injury to the interior. The walls of the windows, on the three sides which face the sea, have been bricked up against the winds of the south and south-west. That is all.'

The ignorant and the credulous, however, are not satisfied. In the first place, the house was not built at the period of the wars of the Revolution. It bears the date '1780,' which was anterior to the Revolution. In the next place it was not built for an observatory. It bears the letters 'ELM-PBILG', which are the double monogram of two families, and which indicate, according to usage, that the house was built for the use of a newly-married couple. Then it has certainly been inhabited: why then should it be abandoned? If the door and windows were bricked up to prevent people entering the house only, why were two windows left open? Why are there no shutters, no window-frames, no glass? Why were the walls bricked in on one side if not on the other? The wind is prevented from entering from the south; but why is it allowed to enter from the north? [*Toilers* I/v/4].

On 21 July 1870 Hugo went with guests on an expedition to Pleinmont. They wanted to see the haunted house by night. They took a ladder and a knife. Having arrived at the house, they propped the ladder against a window, lit the lantern, and entered. They found the interior whitewashed, holes in the flooring of the first storey, timber frames everywhere as new, no weeds, rubble piled up. No spiderwebs, no bats, no night birds. No trace of soot or smoke in the hearth, the flue blocked. [M xiv/1493].

The **Hanois** figures prominently in *The Toilers of the Sea*. Clubin aimed to wreck the *Durande* on the rocks and swim to the coast of Guernsey. His plan went badly wrong – he wrecked the vessel on the Roches Douvres, miles from Guernsey.

In 1860–1862 a lighthouse was erected on the dangerous Hanois rocks. There had been endless debate through the 1850s about who should pay – the States of Guernsey or Trinity House? Eventually work started.

It was built with all the stones dovetailed together laterally and vertically, making the construction a single solid mass. Cornish granite was used, Cornish masons dressed the imported stone on the pier at St Peter Port harbour. The stones were numbered and taken by barge to the site. One such barge may have been a Dutch *schuyt*, the model for Gilliatt's boat in *The Toilers of the Sea*. The foundation stone was laid on 14 August 1860 and the light lit for the first time in November 1862.

If any one person deserved honour for this project, it was Henry Tupper, the French consul in Guernsey. In 1875 French residents in Guernsey presented him with a model of the lighthouse. It can be seen today at the maritime museum at Fort Grey. Tupper was a friend of Hugo. In his own way the novelist paid tribute to the consul by celebrating the benefit of the new lighthouse.

> From the summit of the house, there is a view to the south of the Hanway Rocks, at about a mile from the shore.

> These rocks are famous. They have been guilty of all the evil deeds of which rocks are capable. They are the most ruthless destroyers of the sea. They lie in a treacherous ambush for vessels in the night. They have contributed to the enlargement of the cemeteries at Torteval and Rocquaine.

> A lighthouse was erected upon these rocks in 1862. At the present day, the Hanways light the way for the vessels which

they once lured to destruction; the destroyer in ambush now bears a lighted torch in his hand; and mariners seek in the horizon, as a protector and a guide, the rock which they used to fly as a pitiless enemy. It gives confidence by night in that vast space where it was so long a terror—like a robber converted into a gendarme.

There are three Hanways: the Great Hanway, the Little Hanway, and the Mauve. It is upon the Little Hanway that the red light is placed at the present time.

This reef of rocks forms part of a group of peaks, some beneath the sea, some rising out of it. It towers above them all; like a fortress, it has advanced works: on the side of the open sea, a chain of thirteen rocks; on the north, two breakers—the High Fourquiés, the Needles, and a sandbank called the Hérouée. On the south, three rocks—the Cat Rock, the Percée, and the Herpin Rock; then two banks—the South Bank and the Muet: besides which, there is, on the side opposite Pleinmont, the Tas de Pois d'Aval.

To swim across the channel from the Hanways to Pleinmont is difficult, but not impossible. We have already said that this was one of the achievements of Clubin. The expert swimmer who knows this channel can find two resting-places, the Round Rock, and further on, a little out of the course, to the left, the Red Rock. [*Toilers* I/v/4].

CONCLUSION

When exploring Guernsey today it is easy to fall into misconceptions about the island that Hugo knew. Today Guernsey resembles a garden city. The population is double that of Hugo's day. In the mid 19th century there was 'town' with a population of 16,388 (*1861 Census*); the rest of the population lived in the 9 'country' parishes – an average of 1,491 per parish. Each country parish consisted of a nucleated village clustered around its church. Between one village and the next were fields, farmhouses, more fields. In the 20th century there was a lot of ribbon development along the island roads; the traveller today has little sense of leaving one parish and entering the next. It was far different in the Victorian era. Then, life revolved around the parish. Born in a parish, one attended the parish school, the parish church or chapel, courted a girl of the parish, worked in the parish, married in the parish, raised children in the parish, died in the parish. The next parish was 'foreign.'

Town was distant and different. An enormous mental leap is essential if we are properly to understand the island in the past. The point merits illustration. In 1956 the late Keith Malpas won a scholarship to Elizabeth College in St Peter Port. On his first day at school he befriended a lad from one of the country parishes. This boy was slightly nervous for it was the first occasion in his eleven years of life that he had journeyed to town.

In Hugo's day the country folk generally spoke *patois*; town was partly anglo-phone. The island is small and it is easy to drop into the fallacy of believing that there was a Guernsey patois. In truth the *langue* varied between the patois of the 'high parishes' in the south and the patois of the 'low parishes' in the north. The designation 'high' and 'low' derives from geographical considerations, the contours of the southern parishes are higher than those of the northern parishes. It is, however, true to observe that the patois speakers of the high parishes considered that they spoke a better patois than their low neighbours.

And the subtle variations of patois allowed the keen ear to identify the parish of a speaker. The patois of Torteval and the patois of St Martin's were both 'high' but the one could be distinguished from the other.

Initially we must make a conscious effort to comprehend Guernsey in the 19th century. Thereafter Hugo is an invaluable guide. Virginia Woolf writes about the 'spiritual sovereignty' of novelists such as Scott, the Brontës, George Meredith, and Thomas Hardy –

> They have made the country theirs because they have so interpreted it as to have given it an ineffaceable shape in our minds, so that we know certain parts of Scotland, of Yorkshire, of Surrey, and of Dorset as intimately as we know the men and women who have their dwelling there. Novelists who are thus sensitive to the interpretation of the land are alone able to describe the natives who are in some sense the creatures of the land. [*Times Literary Supplement*, 10 March 1905]

We may add Hugo and Guernsey to Virginia's list. Hugo achieved this 'spiritual sovereignty' in *The Toilers of the Sea*. But he had not managed to incorporate in his novel all that he wished to say about the island and its natives. Hence the addition of his Introduction – *L'Archipel de la Manche* – and it should be read as an integral part of the novel.

ʟɪsᴛ ᴏғ ɪʟʟᴜsᴛʀᴀᴛɪᴏɴs

ABBREVIATIONS

Ansted	Ansted & Latham, *The Channel Islands* (1865)
Barbet	Stephen Barbet, *Map of Guernsey* (1869)
Berry	William Berry, *A History of Guernsey* (1815)
BnF	Bibliothèque nationale de France
GMAG	Guernsey Museum & Art Gallery
GSC	Gregory Stevens Cox collection
Harwood	*Harwood's Illustrations of Guernsey*
Kendrick	T.D. Kendrick, *The Archaeology of the Channel Islands* vol 1 (1928)
Lukis	Lukis Collection, Guernsey Museum & Art Gallery
Metcalfe	*The Channel Islands, historical and legendary sketches, a book of poetry by C J Metcalfe, Jnr.*, London: Simpkin, Marshall and Co., 1852.
PL	Priaulx Library collection
Travailleurs	Victor Hugo, *Les Travailleurs de la Mer* ill. Chifflart (Paris, 1869)
Wimbush	Edith Carey, *The Channel Islands*, ill. Henry Wimbush

143

ᴬCKNOWLEDGEMENTS

Many people have helped and encouraged me over the decades.
I wish to thank Carla McNulty Bauer, Alan Bisson, David de Garis,
Patricia Hands, Jean-Marc Hovasse, Victoria Kinnersly, Jeremy
Smithies, Ken Tough and the officers and members of The Victor
Hugo in Guernsey Society. I am grateful to all who have attended my
Hugo lectures over the decades. Questions and discussions have borne
fruit in this monograph, in the identification of the *basses maisons* for
example. I apologise for not naming all.

Along with Steve Foote, I would like to thank Bibliothèque nationale
de France, Musée d'Orsay, the Priaulx Library and the Guernsey
Museum & Art Gallery for permission to reproduce images from their
collections; as well as Andrew Fothergill, Adrian Bott, Chris George,
Graham Jackson and Michael Paul for their photographs of Guernsey
today.

We would also like to thank Dinah Bott and Roy Bisson of the
Victor Hugo in Guernsey Society, Claire Allen and the Guernsey
Literary Festival committee for inviting us to launch the book at this
year's festivals.

My final thanks are to Steve Foote of Blue Ormer. His patience,
diligence, and enthusiasm are all that any author could pray for – *merci
mille fois!* Any errors that remain are mine alone.

Gregory Stevens Cox
April 2019